ALL ABOUT SHANGHAI AND ENVIRONS

The 1934-35 Standard Guide Book

*With a New Foreword
by Peter Hibbard*

EARNSHAW
BOOKS

ALL ABOUT SHANGHAI AND ENVIRONS

With a new foreword by Peter Hibbard

ISBN-13: 978-988-17621-4-6

All About Shanghai and Environs was first published in 1934.
This edition with a new foreword is reprinted by
China Economic Review Publishing for Earnshaw Books,
Units C&D, 9/F Neich Tower,
128 Gloucester Road, Wanchai, Hong Kong

First printing July 2008
Second printing January 2010
Third printing June 2011

This book has been reset in 10pt Book Antiqua. Spellings and punctuations are left as in
the original edition.

FOREWORD
By Peter Hibbard

THERE are few cities in the world whose name conjures up such evocative images as Shanghai. Since the early 1990s the city has undergone massive social, economic and physical regeneration designed to restore its former status as Asia's centre of trade, finance and commerce. The city's new found affluence is not only embodied in its physical fabric, but also in its indefatigable social exuberance and style that whiffs of the heady speculative years in the early 1930s when the 'Paris of the East' came of age and when *All About Shanghai* was first published.

Before World War II, Shanghai was not one but three cities. Following the Opium War (1839-42) and the signing of the Treaty of Nanking in 1842 the British, closely followed by the Americans and the French, established independent administrative areas where their nationals could reside and trade whilst answering to the laws of their respective nations. In 1863 the British and American areas became one and the 'International Settlement' was born. At its heart was the upcoming 'golden mile' of Asia—the Bund. During its course of development the Bund was transformed from a muddy towpath into an incomparable spectacle of foreign domination with its fine banks, trading houses and other commercial enterprises. The exterior face of its buildings has changed little since the 1930s.

Meanwhile the French Concession, which ostensibly took shape after 1914, developed as a magnificent residential area typified by meandering plane tree-lined avenues, lavish mansions and estates, stylish apartment blocks and theatres. Many of its finer residences were occupied by important Chinese government dignitaries and merchants, as well as by the elites of foreign society. Its French residents numbered but a few and along Avenue Joffre, its main boulevard, a large White Russian community presided over a cavalry of bijou stores and patisseries. The Concession was a playground for underworld activity and political intrigue, and served up a rich cocktail of nefarious pleasures.

In the 1920s and the early 1930s the city's foreign districts acted as a huge playing field for a rapacious band of developers and investors, spearheaded by the legendary British Jew Sir Victor Sassoon. Magnificent shopping streets were created and modern high-rise apartments and hotels sprung up towering over Shanghai's indigenous form of terraced housing. Amidst a cacophony of international styles, thousands of art deco architectural masterpieces were crafted during a period of frenetic growth, comparatively greater in magnitude than that which the city has witnessed in recent times. At the time this guidebook was published in 1934, the city had a population of around three and a half million and was vying with Chicago to stake its claim as the fifth largest city in the world. Of that population, there were only around 80,000 foreigners, with the Japanese and Russians being most prominent amongst them. Most of its population lived in the Chinese-governed Greater Shanghai Municipality that engulfed the International Settlement and the French Concession.

Unashamed in appearance and aspiration Shanghai, slumped on the open-mouthed muddy shores of the Yangtze River, was the only city in Asia that could lay claim to being modern, cosmopolitan, and to being a global player in the world of trade and finance.

Its unique physical, political, economic and cultural identity set it set it apart from any other city in China. It shared much more in common with London, Manchester or New York than it did with Beijing or Guangzhou. As the author of *All About Shanghai* remarks, and he was by no means the first or last, "Shanghai is not China. It is everything else under the sun." So why would tourists from the other side the globe come all the way to see a

China that wasn't 'real'?

Shanghai was a port of call on the first ever round-the-world tour. With some trepidation Thomas Cook, the patriarch of the travel company, left Liverpool on the SS Oceanic in 1872 with a ten-strong group out to discover the 'exoticness' of the Orient. They were not disappointed by the Japanese cities they visited before landing in Shanghai. However as Cook recounted in a letter to *The Times of London,*

> At Shanghai we hastily visited the old Chinese city, which presented a strange contrast to the cities we had just left. Narrow, filthy and offensive streets, choked and almost choking bazaars, pestering and festering beggars in every shape of hideous deformity; sights, sounds, and smells all combined to cut short our promenade of the 'native city' to which no one paid a second visit, and the chief part of our short stay was spent in the English, American or French concessions.

Just five years later a secretary from the British Legation in Peking recounted that he was

> . . . quite unprepared to find such a splendid town. If you can picture to yourself all the large London Clubs and some hundred of the finest city houses transferred to the Thames Embankment you will get an idea of the Bund. In the side streets there are shops similar to those of Bond Street but very much larger.

It was the foreign civility of a place so far from home, in both distance and manner, which provided its main appeal for those seeking solace in an alien land.

Most foreigners staying in the city's hotels in the late nineteenth century were would-be residents who had one particular reason for visiting the city—to make money, and to make it as quickly as possible. Shanghai's resident foreign population, the Shanghailanders, applied the term 'griffin' (previously reserved to describe the fractious behaviour of wild Mongolian ponies) to these newcomers. They would remain so for one year, one month, one week, one day, one hour, one minute and one second after their arrival, before being afforded Shanghailander status. Shanghai's hotels provided a home away from home, a refuge where China was cast in the background. Few tourist pleasure seekers visited the city in those years, though many important dignitaries, for duty or pleasure, including former U.S. President Ulysses S. Grant and Prince George, the future King of England, did pass through the city. In 1892 Thomas Cook included Shanghai on its new annual conducted tour of China and Japan from Australia, as well as offering it as a stop-off for travellers en-route from Australia to America or Europe. They established an office in the city in 1910.

In the early 1920s, Cook's local agency and that of American Express, established in 1918, experienced a huge upsurge in their tourist business as the major shipping lines with their magnificent cruise-liners, including the Belgenland, the Franconia, the Resolute and the Empress of Britain began to call at Shanghai on their circumnavigation of the globe. Cook's were still publicising the familiar international and modern nature of the city as "architecturally comparable to London, Paris and New York," but the native city, which had evoked such a repugnant response from its first group tourists half a century earlier, was now promoted as "of the most picturesque character, presenting the tourist with a rich hunting ground for bargains."

By the time *All About Shanghai* was published the city was regularly playing host to around 40,000, largely rich American, globetrotters each year. Most round-the-world tourists would spend just one or two days in the city and the Shanghailanders had a special name for them as well — 'four-minute guests.'

Many of the larger liners would dock at Woosung (Wusong), near the near the confluence of the Yangtze (Yangzi) and Whangpoo (Huangpu) rivers. Others would dock near the Broadway not far from the Astor House Hotel in the heart of the city. It was not uncommon for four hundred or more eager sightseers to be discharged and relayed in smaller craft to the Bund. Gingerly alighting from their tenders at the Customs Jetty, in front of the Custom House with its clock 'Big Ching' imitating the chimes of Big Ben at Westminster, the European buildings of the Bund would confound the visitor anxiously looking for a fictitious opium-smoking pigtailed China man. They were more likely to bump into a fellow American, wishing to catch up with news from home. As surmised in my book *The Bund Shanghai, China Faces West,* "the Bund presented a Western face to visitors who were usually in some part surprised, bemused, exhilarated or disappointed by its appearance." For many it was their first taste of China and there were no temples or pagodas in sight.

As the author of *All About Shanghai* affirms, the Bund was "the natural starting point for any tour of Shanghai, for it is here that a large majority of newcomers to Shanghai first step foot in the city." The world-girdlers would set off from its promenade in a cavalcade of motor vehicles on carefully crafted itineraries that were designed not to disappoint by presenting images of China in Western-style comfort. Their exhaustive itineraries, apart from sightseeing, took in the sensual delights that were Shanghai's tour de force — shopping, dining, dancing and entertainment. In many ways their Shanghai sojourn was an intensified form of their cruise-ship routine where entertainment during the long sea passages took the form of bridge parties, screenings of the latest talking pictures, games, frolics and contests of all kinds, as well as dancing and masquerades. As such, the sights of Shanghai held little interest for some visitors who were more concerned with hobnobbing and having as much indulgent fun as time would allow. The following sketch printed in the *North-China Herald,* Shanghai's leading British newspaper, nicely summed up the sentiment:

> Yes, Mary Louise, I must say I think a lot more of Shanghai than
> I did when I got on the tender this morning. Why, I almost took

the advice of that Miss Know-it-all who didn't think it worthwhile to come up to the port at all. 'Shanghai's not China' says she. Well maybe not, but there's plenty Chinese here, anyway. And the Cathay Hotel. Can you beat it anywhere? I just loved their dining room and this lounge.

How you ever get time to have your hair marcelled, Mary Louise, in all this excitement! — Oh, you made a date with Captain Williamses wife, and she took you to her favourite hotel, the Palace. Yes, all the Navy people and lots of other folk I met before I sailed told me I must go there if I got the chance. And then after 'elevenses' — do Shanghai people eat every hour of the day? — she took you up to the Bond Street Salon right in the building and you were beautified then and there. And such a smart style, too. I've half a mind to go there instead of seeing the Pagoda this afternoon.

Any way, let's do a little shopping before the party sets out. Will you come along? I've some good addresses. We'll get the clerk to get us some real nice richsha men that can speak American and know where the bargains are.

American Express and Cook's offered an assortment of half-day and full-day tours. The most popular American Express half-day tour commenced with a drive along the International, French and Chinese Bunds to the Native City, where visits were made to the Willow Pattern Tea House and the Mandarin's (Yu) Garden with time for curio shopping in the surrounding maze of crowded lanes. The next stop was at the Convent of Siccawei (Xujiahui) that involved a drive through the French Concession passing the American Community Church and American School, where, of course, many of the American community lived. From there it was a short journey to the Lunghua (Longhua) pagoda and temple before a drive back to town through the classiest thoroughfares of the International Settlement including the Bubbling

Well Road (West Nanjing Road) and past the classy department stores on Nanking Road (East Nanjing Road).

For the affluent tourist of the time there was only one place to head for lunch, or *tiffin* as it was known, and that was the Peking Room on the eighth floor of the Cathay Hotel. The hotel, owned by and second home to Sir Victor Sassoon, was Asia's answer to London's Claridges or New York's Waldorf Astoria — but had a much more playful disposition. The restaurant's interior, which was modelled in the year before this guidebook was published, featured dragon and phoenix motifs in gold relief on its ceilings and elaborate filigree Chinese designs in bronze and plaster based on designs found in the Forbidden City and Temple of Heaven in Beijing. It contained all the treasures that visitors expected to see in China in one room, replete with the all-important modern luxury of air-conditioning.

Many tourists loitered back to the Cathay, or to the Palace Hotel or Astor House Hotel, in the late afternoon to indulge in one of the legendary tea dances that ceremoniously marked the early onset of night fall and a passage to the city's peerless blaze of nightlife. That's when the real sightseeing began. As the author of *All About Shanghai* colourfully describes, "When the sun goes in and the lights come out Shanghai becomes another city, the city of Blazing Night, a night life Haroun-al-Raschid never knew, with tales Scheherezade never told the uxoricidal Sultan Shahriyar."

American Express offered a night tour that began with a feast of sharks' fins and bird's nest soup in a high-class Chinese restaurant, perhaps on Fuzhou Road, followed a visit to the nearby Great World Amusement Centre — an entertainment palace with four floors of stages and booths for plays, acrobatics, singing and feats of magic, as well as penny arcades and galleries of horrors. The next stop was the roof garden at the Sincere department store for Chinese theatricals and sing-song girl performances. The tour ended with revellers being dropped off, just before 11.00 p.m., at one of the city's famous foreign cabarets — the Venus Cafe, Del Montes, the Vienna Gardens or Ciro's; the latter being yet another of Sir Victor Sassoon's interests. Before they stepped off their vehicles they were advised that they were 'on their own now.'

Having survived the dainties of the Chinese menu and the excesses of the night before most female visitors had one thing on their mind in the morning — shopping! For the fashion conscious the most well-known destination of the time was Yates Road (Shimen No. 1 Road) — known to the British as 'the land of a thousand nighties,' and to the Americans as 'pant's alley' on account of its exquisite, but bargain-priced, silk and lace embroidered lingerie. An array of curio stores and an abundance of tailors practised in copying the latest Paris fashions in double-quick time galvanised the street's magnetism for foreign visitors.

Tourists wouldn't have to venture far from the heart of the foreign dominated commercial district around the Bund to experience 'native Chinese life'. As the author highlights on pages 54 and 66, the area to the west of Honan Road (Central Henan Road) was a picturesque Chinese social centre crowded with gaily-decorated restaurants, hotels and places of amusement. Crossing the road one stepped from a modern international financial, social and civic centre, with its skyscraper towers, its cocktails and canapés, its bow ties and handshakes, into a congee of colour, vibrancy and Chinese tradition, of flowing robes, stilettos, soy and of syllabic sounds. It's interesting to note that the road was the first official western boundary of the English Settlement in 1846. By 1848 this boundary had been pushed westwards to the present-day Central Tibet Road and in the 1850s the British, who had originally intended to restrict the area to foreign residents, seized the opportunity of making huge fortunes from the Chinese that had settled there to escape the atrocities of the Taiping Rebellion.

Amongst their other day tours to 'native' districts American Express offered a tour to Minghong (Minhang) to view "typical Chinese canal scenes" that could partly be undertaken on horseback in the company of a dashing ex-officer of the former Imperial Russian Army. A day trip to Pootung (Pudong), a district that was "almost totally neglected by tourists and Shanghai residents," could also be arranged for those wishing to hike though its countryside with its "picturesque villages" and impressive sea dykes.

American Express and Thomas Cook's also offered excursions, of a few days duration, to the neighbouring cities of Soochow (Suzhou), Hangchow (Hangzhou) and the Nationalist Government capital (until 1937) at Nanking (Nanjing); as well as visits to the resorts of Mokanshan (Moganshan) and Pootoo Island (Putuoshan). Recognising that the city wouldn't be the only stop on a foreigner's China itinerary this guidebook includes a substantial chapter not at all about Shanghai, but all about the major tourist spots in China. The distant, but within a day's flying time, northern Chinese cities of Peking (Beijing) and Tientsin (Tianjin), as well as the Yangtsze Gorges (the Three Gorges), are also featured in chapter twelve, *Excursions from Shanghai*.

For those on an organised tour of China, the experience of the modern-day visitor to Shanghai is similar in many ways to that of their 1930s cohorts. They still don't generally stay too long as most itineraries allow just two nights in the city. And despite the obvious backdrop of a new modernity expressed in the faceless walls of the city's glass and steel towers, visitors are still manoeuvred through an intricate passage lined with images of an ancient and 'exotic' China. The historic and perpetually overcrowded Yu Garden, the adjacent Willow Pattern Teahouse, and the engulfing bazaar setting in the faux Old Town (the Native City of old) is still at the heart of all tourist experiences. Many itineraries include visits to one of recently 'restored' water towns such as Zhujiajiao, Wuzhen or Zhouzhuang whose small canals offer an opportunity for a Chinese gondolier ride past traditional single-storey dwellings with white-washed walls, weeping willows and stone-arched bridges. Although few Western tourists now visit the Longhua temple and pagoda, many pay a visit to one of the city's temples, most popularly that of the Jade Buddha. The surviving buildings of the former American School and Church on Hengshan Road may be pointed out if passing by a knowledgeable guide, or may be included on a specialist tour of the former French Concession.

Few venture out to the new commercial centre at Xujiahui unless it's for high-tech shopping or lunch at the former Convent, which has been converted into a Chinese restaurant with a railway carriage diner on its lawn. However the eighth-floor Chinese restaurant of the former Cathay Hotel on the Bund, with its original interior largely intact, remained a popular tourist lunch venue until the north wing of the Peace Hotel, in which it was housed, closed for restoration in 2007.

Although the Bund is no longer a 'natural starting point' for a tour of the city, a visit, even in haste, is an imperative for all visitors to Shanghai. The faces of its buildings that once defined modernity now collectively define 'Old Shanghai.' Many Chinese accounts describe the Bund as a 'museum' or 'gallery' of world architecture. Yet beyond the granite facades chic, modern, international restaurants and bars pull in the crowds after dark. Taking dinner at the legendary *Mon the Bund* is just about as compulsory for today's well-heeled visitor as it was for his 1930s counterpart to dine at the Cathay Hotel. Today most visitors' impressions of Shanghai are sealed on arrival at the futuristic Pudong International Airport and on the journey into the city, either on board the Maglev, the world's first commercial magnetic levitation railway, or on modern highways criss-crossing remnants of urban farmland amidst alien cityscapes designed to dazzle. However that vision of old is being revived at the Shanghai International Cruise Terminal, a stone's throw away from the Bund, which came into operation in 2008.

Shopping is still an important business for the visitor, the shopkeeper and the travel industry in Shanghai. Visitors still pick up their curios and traditional crafts items at the Yu Garden bazaar, while organised tours take in arts and crafts outlets, silk stores and carpet factories. Although a few local fashion stores selling shoddy underwear and pyjamas still survive on Shimen No. 1 Road, the former Yates Road has long fallen from grace much of its 1920s architecture has made way for an international shopping and commercial complex. Hawkers still pester tourists offering a host of counterfeit items and shouts of 'watch, bag' torment or amuse the wise or unwise foreigner strolling along streets in the city's prime tourist haunts.

Although it has not been promoted, or in any way brought to public attention, the recently widened road axis of Central Henan Road (the old Honan Road) is still an important boundary between the former international commercial district extending to the Bund, and the former 'Chinese' district extending to People's Square. Much grand historical architecture still survives in the Bund neighbourhood and comparatively few modern tall buildings are to be found there. With its new skyscraper towers, the area to the west of the road appears at first sight to be much more modern and 'international.' However, wandering off the main thoroughfares the modern-day visitor can still get an idea of what it was like in the 1930s as many colourful small streets lined with two-storey 'shop houses' have somehow deferred their stay of execution. Some buildings on the Fuzhou Road have been dressed in latticework and red lanterns, and many of its stores proffer instruments used in the traditional Chinese arts. A sizeable labyrinth of crowded lanes, which many would describe as putrid, little more than a metre wide and hidden just ten metres behind the stylish shop facades on East Nanjing Road remain to be discovered by the intrepid tourist. Along the road itself the restored, and brightly lit facades of its legendary department stores, originally those of Sincere, Wing On, Sun, and Sun Sun, announce business as usual.

Shanghai's passion for nightlife lives on in the hugely popular karaoke clubs and bars that scatter the city. They can be categorised in the same terms described by the guidebook's author as "high class, low class, or no class." Many of the ballrooms that held so much attraction for those of yesteryear have long since disappeared, though the Paramount Ballroom has been recently revived as a ritzy nightclub and until recently the legendary Peace Hotel Jazz Band filled its dance floor whilst playing renditions of pre-War Swing. The most popular form of evening entertainment for tourists these days is a visit to an acrobatic show, though there are numerous discos and nightclubs for those wishing to dance the night away.

The cities of Hangzhou and Suzhou remain on many tourist itineraries, and with recent improvements in the speed of road and rails links they, along with Nanjing, can all be visited as a day excursion from Shanghai. Moganshan has been resurrected as a fashionable weekend retreat with a small five-star hotel and a British-run lodge, and the beaches and temples of Putuoshan are more popular than ever following the introduction of a fast ferry service from Shanghai.

Although much of the physical fabric of Old Shanghai has been pulverised following the onslaught of redevelopment initiated in the 1980s it may surprise the reader to learn that many of the important buildings and sights described or listed in this guidebook still remain. They may have lost their original functions and names, fallen into disrepair or been altered beyond recognition, but the majority of those buildings occupied by banks, hotels, apartments, clubs, churches, offices, theatres, hospitals and to a lesser extent Chinese places of worship are still there to be stumbled upon by the enquiring sightseer. In fact more Chinese, rather than Western, buildings referred to have been lost since this guidebook was published. Despite the fact that the street names have either changed or are now spelled differently this book can still be gainfully employed to explore downtown Shanghai. To help, a list of old and new street names can be found after the foreword.

The reader of yesteryear could, and the reader of today can, get a quick and useful insight into the chequered history of Old Shanghai from those pages documenting and cataloguing its development. The chapter on *Gods, Legends and Superstitions* also provides an interesting overview of the exoticness of Chinese culture that would not have been much appreciated by the old Shanghailander. A glance at its classified business directory casts some light on the social complexion of a vain and indulgent city.

Look at the number and variety of beauty parlours, dressmakers and tailors listed, among them the Eugene Italian Beauty Parlour, La Parisienne dressmakers and Nee Kee tailors. It's hardly surprising that Shanghai has rekindled its love affair with fashion and vanity today. International fashion houses parade their riches on the city's ritziest strips and seemingly scores of small boutiques and beauty parlours, in various guises, open up every day. Femme fatales are never far from view.

Apart from its value to the visitor this guidebook, as the author points out in the *Foreward*, was written with the griffin and Shanghailander in mind. Moreover it was intended to be a commercial venture aiming to provide a public service and to promote greater profits for Shanghai business. It was essentially a reference work, and from the present-day standpoint contains an interesting snapshot of the might of a great city with its rich mix of statistics on industry, trade, finance, commerce, demography and governance. Some details such as "the number of motor vehicles in Shanghai has increased by 42 per cent in the five years" tamely resonate with the modern Shanghailander. However the only statistics that haven't really changed over the years are those on climate, which is still "not one of the attractions of Shanghai." Overall it provided a handy and readable summary of information that would have had practical value for the foreign resident but was otherwise hidden in the weighty volumes of the Shanghai Municipal Council Annual Report, and in the city's numerous commercial yearbooks and directories.

However, for all its commercial ambition it appears that *All About Shanghai* was not a great business success. Despite its intent to become an annual publication this 1934-35 edition was the only one ever printed. Although it may have made some profit from its numerous adverts, which of course add great spice and interest to this publication for the modern-day reader, it wasn't the first to use adverts in place of subsidy (which is hinted at in the *Foreword*) to produce a guidebook. Early guides to Shanghai such as those published by the Hotel Metropole (1903) and the

Astor House Hotel (1911) also had their pages full of advertising, as did later guides published by Thomas Cook and American Express. *All About Shanghai* also had a direct competitor in the form of *The Shanghai Commercial and Shopping Pocket Guide*, printed in English by a Chinese publisher. It was stacked with advertising, and apart from tourist information for Shanghai and other tourist cities contained an A-Z directory of commercial, public, religious and other enterprises, perhaps making it a more attractive source of reference.

One might also presume that commercial viability would not be a key concern for a publication from *The University Press*. Despite the publishing house's academic title, The University Press had no connection with any university in Shanghai, or indeed anywhere else. It appears that *All About Shanghai* was its first major publication, although the company in the guise of the Oriental Press had been in operation since around 1902. British-born J.A.E. Sanders Bates became managing director of the Oriental Press in 1932 and in the following year his company published their first major compendium, *Men of Shanghai and North China: A Standard Biographical Reference Work*. The preface to the first edition reads:

> As a reference work both here and abroad the publishers believe that this volume will constitute an important addition to the written history of Shanghai, and that it will preserve for the future a distinctly worth-while record of an era of major commercial and political magnitude.

Containing biographies and high quality photos of the most important foreign and Chinese personages in the city, it is now an invaluable resource for serious researchers of Shanghai's modern history and has posthumously fulfilled its ambition. Credit for the work is given to George F. Nellist, an American who was editor-in-chief for the company, which employed just five staff including him. In 1934 the Oriental Press changed its name to The University Press with Nellist remaining on the staff until 1935. Nellist was certainly the man behind the writing of *All About Shanghai* as well as the second and last edition of *Men of Shanghai and North China* in 1935, which again was intended as an annual publication, though his name doesn't appear on either volume.

The prevailing spirit of optimism that exudes from this guidebook reflects the confidence of a city adroit in comfortably riding over its ups and downs and over its setbacks, big and small. With regard to the building industry and its unrelenting profit-laden determination to create a modern city Nellist recounts that despite the serious Sino-Japanese fighting near the International Settlement in 1932, "a tremendous amount of work is always under way, come bad times or good." Given its meteoric rise and its seemingly impenetrable sanctity Shanghailanders expected such conditions to extend into an infinite future. Nellist comments, "What it will be a hundred years from now is a test for the imagination." However, the illusion was torn apart on August 14th 1937 when bombs were dropped on the International Settlement for the first time (inadvertently by Chinese aircraft attempting to hit a Japanese warship) resulting in the death of scores of innocent foreign citizens, and many more Chinese, on the corner of Nanjing Road and the Bund. The Sino-Japanese War had reached Shanghai. Panic-stricken tourists fled the city, never to return, and Shanghai's commercial ambitions and social exuberances were brutally tamed.

It appears that Nellist had already left Shanghai by then and The University Press changed direction in 1938 when it was incorporated under the company ordinances in Hong Kong. By 1940, still in the hands of Sanders Bates, it owned and published a number of Chinese language newspapers, *The Morning Leader, The News Digest* and the *British Evening News* that roused support amongst the Chinese for the British war effort. For those foreigners who returned to Shanghai after World War II, and it appears that Sanders Bates or his company didn't re-emerge, they returned to an alien city, a city of torment, a city of chaos and a city hanging on to life by a slender thread. Old Shanghailanders looked back on the pre-war days and reminisced that the city was never as bad as it was painted to be. Gone were the lines of the International Settlement and the British dominated Shanghai Municipal Council. The British played little or no part in the city that, just a decade earlier, they considered rightfully theirs and *All About Shanghai* had become part of that history itself — an account of another place in another time. Seven decades on this account makes fascinating reading in an age when Shanghai yet again is becoming another place in another time.

Peter Hibbard
Shanghai
June 2008

Street Names

Then	Now	Then	Now
Peking Road	Beijing Lu	Edinburgh Road	Jiangsu Lu
Avenue Road	Beijing Xi Lu	Kiangse Road	Jiangxi Lu
Changle Lu	Changde Lu	Rue du Consulat	Jinling Dong Lu
Rue Bourgeat	Changle Lu	Avenue Foch (East)	Jinling Xi Lu
Rte. de Sayzoong	Changshu Lu	Astor Road	Jinshan Lu
Brenan Road	Changming Lu	Kiukiang Road	Jiujiang Lu
Ward Road	Changyang Lu	Dixwell Road	Liyang Lu
Seward Road	Changzi Dong Lu	Moulmein Road	Maoming Bei Lu
Dalny Road	Dalian Lu	Moulmein Road	Maoming Nan Lu
Broadway	Daming Lu	Bubbling Well Road	Nanjing Xi Lu
Rue Chapsal	Danshui Lu	Columbia Road	Panyu Lu
Point Road	Dinghai Lu	Blvd Deux Republics	Renmin Lu
Seward Road	Dongdaming Lu	Route Pere Robert	Ruijin Er Lu
Broadway East	Dongdaming Lu	Seymour Road	Shaanxi Bei Lu
Route Doumer	Donghu Lu	Carter Road	Shimen Er Lu
Burkhill Road	Fengyang Lu	Rue Montauban	Sichuan Nan Lu
Rte. Pichon	Fenyang Lu	Boundary Road	Tianmu Dong Lu
Route Amiral Coubert	Fumin Lu	Hardoon Road	Tongren Lu
Route G. de Boissezon	Fuxing Xi Lu	Route Magy	Wulumuqi Bei Lu
Rue Lafayette	Fuxing Zhong Lu	Route Louis Dufour	Wulumuqi Nan Lu
Foochow Road	Fuzhou Lu	Jessfield Road	Wanhangdu Lu
Route Cohen	Gaoan Lu	Love Lane	Wujiang Lu
Rue Corneille	Gaolan Lu	Range Road	Wujin Lu
Canton Road	Guangdong Lu	Route Ferguson	Wukang Lu
Rubicon Road	Hami Lu	Rue Moliere	Xiangshan Lu
Avenue Petain	Hengshan Lu	Rue de la Tour	Xiangyang Nan Lu
Wayside Road	Huoshan Lu	Rue Marcel Tillot	Xingang Lu
Avenue Joffre	Huaihai Lu	Rue Paul Henry	Xinle Lu
Avenue Haig	Huashan Lu	Washing Road	Xuchang Lu
Mohawk Road	Huangpi Bei Lu	Avenue Edward VII	Yanan Dong Lu
Baikal Road	Huiming Lu	Great Western Road	Yanan Xi Lu
Museum Road	Huqiu Lu	Avenue Foch (West)	Yanan Zhong Lu
Route Conty	Jianguo Dong Lu	Rue Remi	Yongkang Lu
Rue Chevalier	Jianguo Lu	Route Ghisi	Yueyang Lu
Route J. Frelupt	Jianguo Xi Lu	Chusan Road	Zhoushan Lu

A note from the original publishers:

THE *University Press, publishers of this guide book, specialize in the production of books, magazines, house organs, brochures, and catalogues, with a standard of work equal to that of similar organizations in Europe and America. A highly qualified editorial staff is at the service of clients to advise and assist in the preparation of Mss. Art work of every description is also undertaken. The Press has first-class connexions abroad for the marketing of suitable publications. Inquiries are solicited.*

THE UNIVERSITY PRESS
160 AVENUE EDWARD VII • SHANGHAI

Aerial View of The Bund Business District and Whangpoo River (Courtesy of China National Aviation Corp.)

ALL ABOUT
SHANGHAI

AND ENVIRONS

A Standard Guide Book

Historical and Contemporary Facts
and Statistics

*Illustrated with Maps and
Photographs*

EDITION 1934-35
Price $2.50 (Shanghai Currency)

Published Annually by

THE UNIVERSITY PRESS
160 AVENUE EDWARD VII - SHANGHAI

"Shanghae is by far the most important station for foreign trade on the coast of China. . . . . . .No other town with which I am acquainted possesses such advantages; it is the great gate – the principal entrance, in fact – to the Chinese Empire.

*   *   *

"Taking, therefore, all these facts into consideration – the proximity of Shanghae to the large towns of Hangchow, Soo-chow, and the ancient capital of Nanking; the large native trade, the convenience of inland transit by means of rivers and canals; the fact that teas and silks can be brought here more readily than to Canton; and, lastly, viewing this place as an immense mart for our cotton manufactures, which we already know it to be, – there can be no doubt that in a few years it will not only rival Canton, but become a place of far greater importance."

*   *   *

(Excerpts from *Three Years' Wanderings in the Northern Provinces of China,* by ROBERT FORTUNE, British botanist, who visited Shanghai late in 1843, a few days after the city was declared open to foreign trade on November 17, 1843).

Foreword

IN compiling and publishing *All About Shanghai and Environs,* a Standard Guide Book, The University Press have had no thought of encroaching upon the field of the several very excellent year- and hand-books which are produced here.

All About Shanghai and Environs is designed primarily for the guidance and information of the person who is visiting this city for the first time, although the publishers believe it may be read with interest by many Shanghailanders of long residence. They also believe that it may properly be regarded as the first reasonably complete and adequate Guide Book for the Shanghai area.

The field of service, both to readers and advertisers, is a broad one and is constantly expanding. Shanghai has never made any conscious effort to promote the so-called "tourist industry," as it has been fostered in many other parts of the world, notably California and southern Europe, but the necessities of travel, for both business and pleasure, are each year bringing many thousands of strangers to Shanghai. Their enormous buying power is a marked factor in the prosperity of all business enterprises.

Perfection is an ideal rarely possible of attainment; no claim of perfection is made for this, the first annual edition of *All About Shanghai and Environs.* The publishers are conscious that there may be errors of commission and omission. Constructive criticism for the betterment of subsequent printings of this edition will be welcomed. The scope of future editions will be greatly expanded.

Not the least of the publishers' aims is the performance of a genuinely worthwhile public service for Shanghai, its civic and business interests. Co-operation of others interested in the promotion of this city's welfare and prosperity is invited.

Subsidized guide books have been suggested in the past. The success of this first edition of *All About Shanghai and Environs* proves that a subsidy is not necessary and that a work of merit can be produced on a legitimate business basis.

For their advice and generous help in an editorial advisory capacity grateful acknowledgment is made to Mr. STIRLING FESSENDEN, Secretary General of the Shanghai Municipal Council; Mr. G. BURTON SAYER, Press Information Officer of the S.M.C.; the French Consulate General; Mr. PERCY CHU, Shanghai Bankers' Association; Mr. HUGO SANDOR, Asia Realty Co.; Dr. J. H. JORDAN and Dr. D. J. ALLAN, of the S.M.C. Public Health Department; Mr. C. L. WANG, Postal Remittances and Savings Bank; Mr. A. M. CHAPELAIN, Postal Commissioner; officials of the China National Aviation Corporation, Nanking-Shanghai and Shanghai-Hangchow-Ningpo Railways; and Chinese Government Radio Administration; Mr. H. B. LONGFELLOW, the Robert Dollar Co. and Chairman of the Trans-Pacific Passenger Conference; Mr. GEORGE F. SHECKLEN, R.C.A. Communications, Inc., and Mr. A. MCDERMID, Commercial Pacific Cable Co.

In compiling the book valuable reference sources were found in the *Report of the Hon. Richard Feetham, C.M.G., Judge of the Supreme Court for the Union of South Africa, to the Shanghai Municipal Council; The Encyclopaedia Sinica,* edited by Mr. SAMUEL COULING, M.A. (Edin.); *A Short History of Shanghai,* by Dr. F. L. HAWKS POTT; *The History of Shanghai,* by G. LANNING and S. COULING; *Historic Shanghai,* by C. A. MONTALTO DE JESUS; *The China Year Book,* edited by Mr. H. G. W. WOODHEAD, O.B.E.; *Handbook for China,* compiled and edited by Mr. CARL CROW; *China Industrial Handbooks,* published by the Bureau of Foreign Trade of the Ministry of Finance; *Statistics of Shanghai,* compiled by the Shanghai Civic Association, and various publications of the Whangpoo Conservancy Board.

THE PUBLISHERS.

Contents

Masonic Club — American University Club — Rotary
Club — Women's Clubs — Y.M. and W.C.A.'s — Golf —
Riding — Paper-hunting.
MILADY GOES A'SHOPPING — Information on Jade — Silks and
Furs — Modern Women.

New Zealand—Coast and River Routes—Distances From
Shanghai.

MAPS AND ILLUSTRATIONS

Chapter One
HISTORICAL BACKGROUND

S Shanghai, sixth city of the World!
Shanghai, the Paris of the East!
Shanghai, the New York of the West!
Shanghai, the most cosmopolitan city in the world, the fishing village on a mudflat which almost literally overnight became a great metropolis.

Inevitable meeting place of world travellers, the habitat of people of forty-eight different nationalities, of the Orient yet Occidental, the city of glamorous night life and throbbing with activity, Shanghai offers the full composite allurement of the Far East.

Not a wilderness of temples and chop-sticks, of jade and pyjamas, Shanghai in reality is an immense and modern city of well-paved streets, skyscrapers, luxurious hotels and clubs, trams, buses and motors, and much electricity.

Less than a century ago Shanghai was little more than an anchorage for junks, with a few villages scattered along the low, muddy banks of the river. What it will be a hundred years from now is a test for the imagination. Principal gateway to China, serving a hinterland population of more than 200,000,000, many close observers believe it will become the largest city in the world.

Early History.—Although neighbouring cities like Nanking, Soochow, and Hangchow figure spaciously in the chronicles of ancient China, Shanghai is very rarely mentioned. It undoubtedly formed part of the Kingdom of Wu (B.C. 513), a great feudal state that embraced the modern province of Kiangsu, in which Shanghai is situated, but the connection is not recorded. The earliest reference to what is now Shanghai is placed at approximately B.C. 200, when it was called "Hu-tuh" and known as a fishing station. From that remote date until A.D. 1280, when it acquired the name of Shanghai ("Above the Sea"), there is a marked hiatus in the historical record.

In 1554 Shanghai attained the status of a "Walled Town." The wall is stated to have been from three to four miles long and twenty-three feet in height, with six gates and twenty arrow towers. Its principal purpose was to ward off attacks by Japanese pirates, who at that period frequently raided and pillaged the coastal towns of China. The last remnants of the wall disappeared after the Revolution in 1911. The Shanghai of the 16th century was notable in another way. It was the birthplace of Lu Tsih and Wang Ke, two of China's greatest writers, and Hsu Kwang-ch'i, friend and pupil of Matteo Ricci, the Jesuit missionary.

There is nothing of outstanding importance to relate about Shanghai from the dawn of the 17th century down to 1843, when it was opened to foreign trade.

Coming of the Foreigners.—What was probably the first definite attempt to open Shanghai to foreign trade came in 1832 when Mr. Hugh Hamilton Lindsay was entrusted with a commercial mission to the North from Macao by the East India Company. He was denied entrance to Amoy, Foochow, and Ningpo, but succeeded in obtaining a hearing by Chinese authorities at Shanghai. The decision, however, was that foreign trade should be restricted to Canton. In a report of his voyage Mr. Lindsay said Shanghai had great possibilities as a commercial centre. He was right.

Friction over trade relations at Canton culminated in a conflict between Great Britain and China, the so-called "Opium War," 1840-43, and one result of this war was the birth of modern Shanghai. In the course of their operations the British sent a combined naval and military expedition to the North, captured Amoy, Ningpo and Chapoo, forced the Woosung forts and a landing party entered a district now included in the International Settlement.

Treaty Ports Opened. — Pressing their way up the Yangtsze river, the British reached Nanking and the Treaty of Nanking was signed on board a British warship, August 29, 1842. The most important provision of this pact between Great Britain and China was that Canton, Amoy, Foochow, Ningpo and Shanghai were to be opened to foreign trade, the "Treaty Ports," as they became known. Formal declaration that Shanghai was open to foreign trade was made on November 17, 1843, following ratification of the treaty.

It is interesting to note that in this original treaty no definite provision was made for territorial acquisitions, but it was clearly provided that within the Treaty Ports "British subjects with their families and establishments shall be allowed to reside for the purpose of carrying on their mercantile pursuits, without molestation or restraint."

Following closely on the British action, the United States and France by treaties signed on July 3, 1844, and October 24, 1844, respectively, acquired the right of trade by their nationals in the Treaty Ports. Thus, in effect, all of China was opened to foreign commerce. Great Britain, the United States and France were thereafter known as the "Treaty Powers."

In its early development the boundaries of the original Foreign Settlement were the old Yang King Pang creek (now covered by Avenue Edward VII) to the South, the Whangpoo river on the East, what is now Peking Road on the North and, on the West, Barrier Road (now Honan Road), enclosing an area of 138 acres.

French Concession. — The nucleus of the present French Concession was created April 6, 1849, when the first Consul for France at Shanghai, M. Montigny, reached an agreement with the Chinese authorities for the creation of a defined district which should be under French government. The area was 164 acres.

France has ever since exercised exclusive control over its own Concession. A proposal to unite the French Concession and the International Settlement was once brought forward but failed to receive the approval of France.

Americans Join British.—It is impossible to give an exact or definite account of the formation of the original American Settlement, that section of the present International Settlement lying North of Soochow Creek and including the present Hongkew district, for it was a natural, not a political growth, caused by an expansion or overflow from the old Foreign (British) Settlement.

The American Settlement was really founded in 1848, when the American Episcopal Church Mission, under the direction of Bishop William J. Boone, the first Anglican Bishop in China, was established North of Soochow Creek, in Hongkew. Hongkew then was low and swampy, with the present Broadway the foreshore of the Whangpoo river. The United States Consul to Shanghai, raised the American flag in the district in February, 1854.

A natural community of interests resulted in the union of the British and American Settlements in 1863, and the concurrent birth of the present International Settlement.

WARS AND ALARUMS

Throughout the ninety years of its occupation by foreigners Shanghai has frequently been the centre or a major theatre of stressful military and political action. That during this brief period, as history is measured, Shanghai, despite the many crises it has faced, has developed from a village into one of the world's principal metropoles is sufficient proof of the inherent virility of this youngest of the great cities. Being a Guide Book, not a history, this section must necessarily be brief.

The Taiping Rebellion, bringing to China one of its most terrible scourges, had its inception in Canton in 1851. A group of rebels known as the "Small Swords" fought their way northward to Shanghai and on September 7, 1853, entered and captured the Chinese City and held it until February 17, 1855. During this period of almost constant fighting between the Imperialists and rebels the Foreign Settlement remained neutral and, except for irregular and occasional violations, maintained its territorial integrity.

Volunteer Corps Formed. — As a precautionary measure of defense, when it appeared that fighting was inevitable, representatives of Great Britain, the United States and France, meeting on April 12, 1853, authorized the organization of a volunteer corps. This was the birthday of the present splendidly efficient Shanghai Volunteer Corps, which on many subsequent occasions has protected the city.

The Volunteers received their first real baptism of fire on April 4, 1854, when, operating with British and American naval parties, and unexpectedly reinforced by Chinese rebels, they dislodged a large force of Imperialists from a threatening position near the western boundary of the Settlement. This engagement, known as the "Battle of Muddy Flat," was fought at what is now the Race Course and Public Recreation Ground, in the heart of Shanghai.

Customs Service Supervised. — Another important development of this period of governmental instability was the re-organization of the customs service under foreign supervision, undertaken by representatives of Great Britain, the United States and France, the three Treaty Powers, with the concurrence of the local Chinese authorities.

The re-opening of the Custom House on July 12, 1854, may be said to mark the birth of the present admirably conducted Chinese Maritime Customs service.

Taipings Menace City. — The "Small Swords," expelled from the Chinese City by a joint action of French and Imperialist forces, were never recognized by the Taipings but their incursion was part of the general revolutionary movement. Shanghai had a brief breathing spell but the Taiping Rebellion soon had spread over most of northern China and there was almost constant fighting during the period 1860-64. (Details of this and other periods in Shanghai's history may be obtained from the works mentioned in the Foreword to this book).

With the capture of Soochow by the Taiping rebels in June, 1860, Shanghai was again faced by a deadly menace. The situation had been further complicated by the second war between Great Britain and China, 1856-60, in which France was allied with the British, but which had slight direct bearing on Shanghai. On August 17, 1860, the rebels attacked Shanghai but found the city stoutly defended by British and French forces, the Volunteers, and foreign warships in the Whangpoo. There was desultory, long range fighting but the foreign settlements were not invaded.

"Ever Victorious Army." — At this juncture, in a concerted effort to suppress the Taiping Rebellion, one of the romantic figures of history appeared, Frederick Townsend Ward, a New England (American) shipmaster, who organized the "Ever Victorious Army," composed of foreigners and loyalist Chinese. Ward, commissioned a General by the Imperial government, led his forces in many engagements against the Taipings and was killed in action near Ningpo, September 21, 1862. His memory is still revered by the Chinese.

Ward was succeeded by a lieutenant, one Henry A. Burgevine, who soon faded out of the picture, and command of the "Ever Victorious Army" came to Charles George Gordon ("Chinese Gordon"), a British army officer. Gordon's aggressive campaign broke the Taiping Rebellion by May, 1864, and the "Ever Victorious Army" was disbanded. The rebellion ended entirely in 1865.

Ward and "Chinese Gordon." — Historians differ widely in their evaluation of the character and services of the American, General Ward, but it is noteworthy that Gordon paid him a very eloquent tribute as a man and a soldier. "Chinese Gordon," as he was afterward known, served Great Britain brilliantly in North Africa and died in the defense of Khartum against the Mahdi, January 26, 1885, a gallant gentleman and officer. It is not unreasonable to assume that the joint efforts of Ward and Gordon saved Shanghai from destruction during the Taiping Rebellion.

Ward's career was a stormy one. During his early military service for the Imperialists he was summoned before the American Consul in Shanghai, charged with inducing the desertion of British and American sailors, many of whom, attracted by the promise of adventure and high pay, and perhaps loot, had joined his "Ever Victorious Army." Presumably to avoid trial, Ward renounced his American citizenship and became a subject of the Emperor.

Later, however, both British and Americans welcomed the help of Ward's army in keeping the Taipings out of Shanghai and he was hailed as a hero.

Waged with the utmost ferocity by both Imperialists and rebels, the Taiping Rebellion (1851-65) ravaged eleven of the richest provinces of China and caused the death of 20,000,000 people.

It is a grotesque fact that the years of the Taiping Rebellion proved a temporary boon to Shanghai, for from the influx into the foreign settlements of Chinese refugees there resulted an

enormous increase in population and property values, and necessarily, subsequent extension of the settlements' boundaries. There was a marked recession in population later, it is true, but permanent gains were made.

Minor Troubles. — For many years following the Taiping Rebellion, save for minor internal and major external disturbances which exercised slight effect, Shanghai enjoyed a period of growth and comparative tranquility.

There were the Ningpo Guild riots in the French Concession in 1874, in which the Chinese registered their opposition to the creation of a road through a cemetery; the French and Chinese war, 1881-85, growing out of a dispute over trade routes through Annam, which had no repercussions in Shanghai; the anti-missionary demonstrations in the Yangtsze valley in 1891; the Sino-Japanese war of 1894, from which Shanghai was entirely excluded as a theatre of operations, although a certain degree of apprehension was felt, and the rioting of April 5, 1897, when the Shanghai Municipal Council increased the license tax on wheelbarrows.

The "Plague Riots" occurred on November 10, 1910, resulting from opposition to the enforcement of Public Health by-laws for the prevention of plague.

Boxer Uprising. — A strong anti-foreign spirit developed in 1899 and culminated in the Boxer troubles of 1900. The story of the siege and relief of the Peking Legations is too well known to require exposition. Shanghai was apprehensive but was not menaced.

Purely local, and serious, trouble came on December 8, 1905, however, through agitation over decisions and jurisdiction of the Mixed Court. Rioters attacked and set fire to the Louza Police Station, which later was to figure in a much more important incident. The police in this instance were under instructions not to shoot. Eventually the situation was placed under control by the police, Shanghai Volunteers, and naval landing parties. There were several casualties.

Revolution. — In October of 1911 the Republican Revolution, promoted for years by Dr. Sun Yat-sen, came to a head. Shanghai was in no way affected by the fighting and the Chinese of the Shanghai area accepted the new regime by acclamation on November 4.

A real crisis came in the Summer of 1913, however, during the so-called "second revolution," directed against the government of Yuan Shih-kai. On July 20 revolutionists attempted to seize the Chinese Telegraphs in Shanghai and were successfully resisted by the municipal police as military operations within the Settlement were considered a violation of its neutrality.

There was considerable fighting in the Chinese districts adjacent to the French Concession and the International Settlement and for a week there was a nightly serenade of shells passing over sections of foreign-governed territory. The Shanghai Volunteer Corps was mobilized and foreign naval forces were landed.

The outbreak of the World War in 1914 brought new problems. Shanghai was not directly concerned, but many young Shanghailanders returned to their native countries for military service, and, particularly after China's declaration for the Allies, German interests inevitably suffered greatly.

Crisis of 1924-25. — Warfare between factions in Kiangsu and Chekiang provinces, an outgrowth of differences between the Fengtien-Anfu and Chihli political parties, created a new and disturbing situation in the latter months of 1924 and the early part of 1925. It was feared that possession of Shanghai was coveted by both factions.

A state of emergency existed for several months. The Shanghai Volunteer Corps was again mobilized, naval forces were landed, and the French Concession and the International Settlement, under a joint defense plan, were barricaded. Thousands of Chinese refugees again poured into the foreign settlements.

Ten thousand fugitives from the defeated army were disarmed within the French Concession and International Settlement.

Bloody Riot of May 30, 1925. — The interlude of peace for

VIEW OF THE BUND, ABOUT 1889

Shanghai was of brief duration, Strong labour agitation, which had been developing for some months, reached a bloody climax on May 30, 1925, when a number of Chinese, who were making a street demonstration, were arrested and confined in the Louza Police Station. Sympathizers gathered in large numbers and demanded their release. The police opened fire. Four Chinese were shot dead and four of the wounded died later.

Feeling ran high. A strong anti-foreign movement gathered momentum. A general strike was declared on May 31. There were frequent clashes between the Chinese and the police. It is stated that 24 Chinese were killed and 36 wounded during the trouble. On June 1 the Shanghai Municipal Council declared a state of emergency and the Shanghai Volunteer Corps was called out.

From the Chinese came an insistent demand for the abolition of extraterritoriality and the return to Chinese sovereignty of all foreign concessions. International diplomacy was invoked before a settlement was finally reached. Perhaps the most important immediate outcome of this unfortunate incident was the eventual inclusion of Chinese representatives on the Shanghai Municipal Council, which, however, was not effected until April 20, 1928.

Nationalists Advance. – The Nationalist movement, fostered in Canton, launched a military expedition to the North in July, 1926. The Nationalists swept away all opposition in their advance through Central China to Hankow. The British returned to the Chinese their concessions at Hankow and Kiukiang. Shanghai sensed a fresh menace to the integrity of its international character.

Early in 1927, British, American, Japanese, French, Italian, Dutch and Spanish forces were brought into the city. The Shanghai Volunteer Corps was again on active duty. The Nationalist forces began their advance on Shanghai in February.

Shanghai was disturbed by labour disorders, currently reported to have been fomented by Communists within the Nationalist ranks. The subsequent expulsion of the communistic influences is a matter of history.

Shanghai An Armed Camp.—Through the activities of the foreign forces and the Shanghai Volunteer Corps, the French Concession and the International Settlement were made one armed camp, barricaded by barbed wire entanglements. The curfew was invoked. Residents not required for urgent duty were excluded from the streets from 10 p.m. until 4 a.m. each night.

The Nationalists took the Chinese sections of Shanghai and there was some fighting in Chapei and the Chinese City, but no organized or official attempt was made to violate the foreign settlements. This situation, at the moment, appeared to be the most critical with which Shanghai had yet been confronted, but five years later the city was to undergo its heaviest baptism of modern artillery fire. Five thousand of the defeated Northern troops, seeking refuge, were interned in the International Settlement.

Sino-Japanese Fighting.—There has been friction between the Japanese and the Chinese since the war of 1894. Japanese military operations in Manchuria in the Fall of 1931 intensified the anti-Japanese feeling in China and a series of incidents were brought to a head in January-February, 1932, when the Japanese landed strong naval units to eject Chinese military forces (the 19th Route Army) from the Chapei district. There is a large Japanese population in the Hongkew district of the International Settlement, adjacent to Chapei.

There was almost constant fighting for a month and again Shanghai residents had their nightly thrill from the roar of heavy gun fire. The Chinese finally retired but much of the Chapei district had been reduced to ruins.

During this Sino-Japanese "undeclared war" Great Britain and the United States strongly reinforced their Shanghai garrisons, the Shanghai Municipal Council again declared a state of emergency and enforced the 10-to-4 curfew, and the Shanghai Volunteer Corps was again under arms. Shanghai was a military zone for a month. But there was no actual fighting in defense of the foreign settlements.

[12]

So, wars come and go, but through the ninety years of its modern existence, Shanghai, although faltering at times, has never really been out of stride in its advance to its inevitable destiny.

*　　*　　*

Nanking Road was known to early residents as "Park Lane," The Bund as "Yangtsze Road," Szechuen Road as "Bridge Street," Kiangse Road as "Church Street," Canton Road as "North-gate Street," and Peking Road as "Consulate Road."

*　　*　　*

Mr S. Clifton, first Superintendent of Police for Shanghai, had an onerous post. In addition to his duties as police officer, he was called upon to supervise the cleaning and lighting of the streets, to assist in the laying down of roads and the collection of taxes, to abate nuisances and keep a check on arms brought into the Settlement, to remove obstructions and give assistance to Consuls when they needed it. Being a married man, Mr. Clifton was graciously allowed to spend his spare moments in the bosom of his family.

Chapter Two
GOVERNMENTS OF SHANGHAI

THE city of Shanghai is governed by three separate and distinct municipal entities, the International Settlement, the French Concession, and the City Government of Greater Shanghai, the last named exclusively administered by Chinese and including all sections of the city outside of the two foreign settlements.

The original formation of the International Settlement and the French Concession has been touched upon in Chapter One. In this chapter a brief outline of the territorial and political development of the three administrative units of Shanghai will be given.

The City Government of Greater Shanghai, theoretically, controls an area of 320 square miles, including territory on both sides of the Whangpoo river, but it is not all yet under an administrative municipal organization. This great area compares with 12.66 square miles, jointly, for the International Settlement and French Concession.

The first definite boundaries of the Foreign Settlement were determined by an agreement between the British and Chinese, dated September 20, 1846, and enclosed an area of approximately 830 mow, or 138 acres. An agreement of November 27, 1848, increased the area to 470 acres.

Incorporation of the sprawling American Settlement by the agreement reached with the British September 21, 1863, added 1,309 acres, the boundaries having been determined by U.S. Consul George F. Seward and the Chinese on June 25, 1863. Two extensions, through negotiations with the Chinese, added sections of 1,896 and 1,908 acres, respectively, in 1899, bringing the present total area of the Settlement to 33,503 mow, or 5,583 acres.

The original French Concession, under agreement of April 6,

1849, comprised 164 acres, increased by 23 acres on October 29, 1861; 171 acres, January 27, 1900, and, a tremendous gain, 2,167 acres on July 20, 1914, the present total area being 15,150 mow, or 2,525 acres; rather less than one-half of the Settlement area.

INTERNATIONAL SETTLEMENT

As at present constituted, executive direction of the government of the International Settlement is vested in the Shanghai Municipal Council. The chief active executive officer is the Secretary General, a salaried official appointed by the Council, a position occupied since April, 1929, by Mr. Stirling Fessenden, an American lawyer and a former Chairman of the Council.

The Council, none of whose members is paid, is now composed of fourteen, including, at this writing, five British, two Americans, two Japanese, and five Chinese, who choose their own Chairman. The foreign members are elected annually by the Ratepayers (tax-payers). The Chinese are chosen by Chinese residents. There is no specification as to the nationalistic complexion of the foreign group, its present composition being the result of what might be termed an "unwritten law." Chinese representation, however, is limited to five members.

"Land Regulations." — The basic foundation of the civic government is embodied in a code known as the "Land Regulations," first promulgated by Captain George Balfour, first British Consul, November 29, 1845. This code, which has been subjected to numerous revisions, may be regarded as the Magna Carta or bill of rights of Shanghai, as it defines the boundaries of the Settlement, provides for the acquisition and lease of lands (originally in perpetuity from the Chinese), defines the qualifications of electors, who must be land owners or taxpayers, and otherwise provides a structure for administrative government. One historian says the Land Regulations "formed the basis of subsequent enactments governing the Settlement." It is interesting to note that under the suffrage arrangement the annual vote, determining the executive personnel of the government, does not exceed 2,000.

SHANGHAI MUNICIPAL COUNCIL: *Standing, from left:* Judge John C. Wu, *Adviser on Municipal Affairs;* Stirling Fessenden, *Secretary-General,* and Councillors E. Y. B. Kiang, J. H. Liddell, J. W. Carney, E. F. Harris, Judge C. S. Franklin, O. Okamoto and Singloh Hsu; J. R. Jones, *Secretary. Seated, from left:* Councillors P. W. Massey, Yu Ya-ching, Brig.-Gen. E. B. Macnaghten, H. E. Arnhold, *Vice-Chairman;* T. Funatsu, and L. T. Yuan. *Inset:* A. D. Bell, *Chairman. Absent:* Councillors Pei Tsuyee, F. J. Raven, and T. D. Woo.

Control of Legislation. — In addition to the annual election of the Councillors, the Ratepayers meet once a year (special meetings may be called by petition) to receive and approve or criticize, the annual report of the Council, pass the budget for the next year and consider other civic matters, frequently suggesting enactments to be made by the Council.

Thus, in theory, the Ratepayers originate, and the Council executes, but any amendment to the Land Regulations is subject to international negotiation and to acceptance by the Chinese government; the by-laws of the municipality may be amended or added to by resolution of a special meeting of the Ratepayers and with the approval of a majority of the Consuls and Ministers of the Treaty Powers (now the fourteen foreign nations enjoying extraterritoriality) — *see* section in this chapter, "Privileges of Foreigners").

International Tendency. — Land privileges in the original Foreign (British) Settlement were at first regarded as applying only to the British, but in 1851, by Chinese authority, merchants of all nations were permitted to build in the Settlement, then administered chiefly by a "Committee of Land Renters."

An elective Municipal Council was authorized and its first meeting was held on July 11, 1854. New Land Regulations, promulgated in that year, were signed by the Consuls of the three original Treaty Powers, Great Britain, France and the United States, thus giving the first suggestion of "International" to the scope of the foreign settlements, although the indication thus given of an amalgamation of French interests was not fulfilled (*see* "French Concession" in this chapter).

The decision to unite the British and American settlements was reached at a meeting on September 21, 1863, when land renters of the foreign settlements, except the French, agreed to pool their interests and form "The International Settlement of Shanghai," the Ministers of the Treaty Powers approving this decision, and the actual fusion of territorial interests was consummated in December, 1863, one of the provisions being that the Americans agreed to pay one-half of the policing costs of the new community.

As before stated, there were never any formal negotiations between the Chinese and Americans for the creation of the original "American Settlement," but its boundaries, before incorporation with the British, had been defined by joint agreement of Mr. George F. Seward, the American Consul, and Chinese authorities in 1863. Consul Seward was one of the first to propose the formation of one government for both settlements, American and British. As historians say, the American Settlement "just growed." Justification for the Settlement, however, may be found in the fact that by treaty China had extended to Americans the same privileges to acquire lands for residence and business purposes as the British and French enjoyed.

Chinese Join Settlement. — The Foreign Settlement originally was exclusively for foreigners, but Chinese, seeking refuge during the Taiping Rebellion in the early sixties and subsequent external disorders, were permitted to enter and many remained.

Because of the additional administrative burdens thus imposed it was found necessary to subject these Chinese to taxation but they had no direct representation in local government until 1928 when three Chinese members were added to the Municipal Council and in 1930 the membership was increased to five. The inclusion of Chinese Councillors was a direct outcome of the agitation following the bloody rioting of May 30, 1925 (*see* Chapter One).

"Free City" Proposed. — It is of historical interest, because of the tremendous potential changes it might have made in the destiny of Shanghai, to note that in 1862, during the general chaos created by the Taiping Rebellion, the Municipal Council brought forward a plan to make Shanghai a "free and independent city," not an open port, like Hongkong (British), but in reality a municipal republic, entirely self-governing. The system of suffrage proposed would have given control of the city to property owners, both Chinese and foreign.

The foreign Consuls and Ministers, however, took a negative attitude, especially the British representatives. Mr. W. H. Medhurst, British Consul to Shanghai, said: "The territory belongs to the Emperor of China, who merely accords foreign powers, that have entered into treaties with himself, an extraterritorial jurisdiction over their own citizens resident in this port (Shanghai), but retains for himself all authority over his own territory and subjects."

The British Minister to China, Sir Frederick Bruce, was even more emphatic in his opposition. He said: "The English concession at Shanghai is neither a transfer nor a lease of the land in question to the British Crown, the land so acquired remaining Chinese territory."

The International Settlement (considered as a community of identic civic interests and services) is now stretching beyond its boundaries and overflowing into Chinese territory that is under the supreme jurisdiction of the City Government of Greater Shanghai, but in recent years the Chinese authorities have refused further territorial extensions, presumptively in the expectation of the ultimate abolition of extraterritorial privileges.

It should be noted here that the official point of view of the City Government of Greater Shanghai, according to the Feetham Report, is that the International Settlement and French Concession actually form part of the area of the Chinese municipality, though distinguished from other parts of that area as "special areas," and that while the exercise of authority by the Chinese municipal government is subject for the present to practical limitations in respect of these special areas, its bureaux are for certain administrative purposes entitled to exercise direct authority within the Settlements.

Extra-Settlement Roads.—Congestion has forced foreigners to take up residence along 48 miles of extra-Settlement (outside the Settlement boundaries) roads which have been constructed by the Municipal Council under powers of acquisition granted by the Land Regulations. Two fine parks have also been provided by the Council outside of the Settlement under the same authority. There has been some friction between Settlement and Chinese authorities over the policing of extra-Settlement roads and the extensions of public utilities.

Administrative functions of the government of the International Settlement, as in all other large modern cities, are executed by departments, such as Health, Public Works, Police, Fire, etc., the chiefs being appointed by the Council.

FRENCH CONCESSION

The comparative brevity of this section is not due to editorial neglect, but rather to the fact that the French Concession since its inception has been virtually free from the complexities of governmental development which have marked the history of the International Settlement because of the latter district's intricate international composition. Part of its history, also, has already been covered in preceding sections.

The French Concession is also under the management of a Municipal Council, much like the International Settlement, and operates with the usual departments or bureaux for the direct administration of civic business. But there is an important difference in the fact that the resident French Consul General is the supreme local authority, exercising the power of veto over the council's actions. He is answerable only to the French Minister to China and to the French Government.

The Council, of which the Consul General is the President, also includes a Vice President and sixteen Councillors. The Consul General and the Vice President, of course, are French. At this writing the Councillors include nine French, five Chinese and two British subjects.

The Feetham Report of 1931 said: "French Concession, administered by the French Consul General, with the assistance of an advisory body consisting partly of appointed foreign members, and partly of Chinese members chosen by Chinese organizations."

Since that time, there has been a further concentration of local authority in the hands of the Consul General, who now selects all members of the Council.

Original Concession Small. — The original French Concession was not larger in area than the present Race Course and Public Recreation Ground of the International Settlement.

The development of the French Concession, particularly as a residential district, has been very rapid in the past few years.

Because of congestion in the International Settlement many foreigners who conduct their businesses there, have their homes in the French Concession. However, a large and flourishing business district is developing in the Avenue Joffre section.

Union of Settlements Blocked. — The French Consul, in concurrence with the British and American Consuls, signed the second code of Land Regulations in 1854, and for a period thereafter, at least in theory, the three foreign settlements were under a rather loosely applied joint administration, to the extent of the provisions of the Regulations.

This action was never ratified by the French Government, however, and in effect the French have always exercised solitary control over their own Concession, which has come to be regarded as French territory. The first French Municipal Council was formed on May 1, 1862, and a Code of Municipal Regulations was published in July, 1866.

CITY GOVERNMENT OF GREATER SHANGHAI

The first efforts toward the organization of a municipal form of government in the Chinese-controlled territory adjacent to the French Concession and the International Settlement was made in 1911, following the republican Revolution which overthrew the Manchu Dynasty. Little progress was made, however, until July 7, 1927, when, at the triumphant conclusion of the Nationalist movement, the City Government of Greater Shanghai was formally established.

The government consists of a Secretariat and eight bureaux: Social Affairs, Public Safety, Finance, Public Works, Education, Public Health, Land, and Public Utilities. The chief executive is the Mayor, appointed by the Central Government at Nanking, and the government functions under the direct control of the Executive Yuan of the Central Government without the intervention of any provincial authority.

Progressive Movements.—General Wu Te-chen, a distinguished Chinese soldier and political leader, was appointed Mayor on January 1, 1932, and at this writing still occupies the office. His services have been of the highest order. Shortly after

---

he assumed office the Sino-Japanese "undeclared war" broke out and Mayor Wu carried through that difficult period with distinction. To his enterprising leadership goes much credit for the rebuilding of the destroyed Chapei district.

The City Government of Greater Shanghai is constructing a magnificent new civic centre to the northeast of the International Settlement and ambitious plans have been made and are being executed for extensive industrial and port development in the entire area between Woosung and Shanghai, a project the completion of which will do much to relieve the growing pressure on the shipping and commercial facilities of the foreign settlements.

PRIVILEGES OF FOREIGNERS

There has been much misunderstanding of the term "extraterritoriality." Briefly defined, in present usage it means a treaty arrangement whereby a nation acquires exclusive jurisdiction, in both civil and criminal matters, over its recognized citizens residing in a foreign country. Thus, for example, if a Chinese sues an American in Shanghai, he must do so in the United States Court. If an American sues a Britisher he must apply to the British court.

Extraterritoriality in China may be said to date from the Treaty of Nanking in 1842, when British consular officials were authorized to arbitrate and settle the differences of their nationals with Chinese. However, there was not a definite statement of the principles of extraterritoriality as they were subsequently accepted. There was a much clearer and more concise definition of the principles involved in the treaty which the United States negotiated with China in 1844 (*see* Chapter One).

Favoured Nations. — Fourteen foreign nations, signatories to "favoured nations" treaties with China, exercise extraterritorial privileges and rights in Shanghai.

They are the United States, Belgium, Brazil, Great Britain, Denmark, France, Italy, Japan, The Netherlands, Norway, Por-

S.M.C. ADMINISTRATION BUILDING

tugal, Spain, Sweden and Switzerland. These either have their own national courts or Consular courts. For instance, the British in Shanghai have H.B.M. Supreme Court and the Americans the United States Court for China. All other foreign tribunals are Consular Courts, presided over by the Consul Generals of the countries concerned, except in the case of France, Italy, and Japan, by whom judges are especially appointed.

Nations represented in Shanghai which have no extraterritorial rights are Russia, Germany, Austria and Hungary. Nationals of these countries, and other unrecognized foreigners, are subject to the jurisdiction of Chinese courts, of which there are two in the International Settlement. The Shanghai Municipal Council has the right to sue in any court.

Chinese Courts.—Chinese residing in the International Settlement are under the jurisdiction of the two Chinese Provisional Courts, the Shanghai Special Area District Court and a "Second Branch" of the Kiangsu Province High Court.

The problem of dealing with Chinese offenders in the Settlement has been a vexatious one, the present system having come into effect in 1930. From 1864 to 1927 there was a Mixed Court for Chinese not resident of their own "Native City." This was originally established for the trial of cases in which foreigners were involved but later came to include cases of all Chinese, whether or no foreigners were involved who came under the jurisdiction of the International Settlement. In the old Mixed Court the Chinese magistrate was assisted, in turn, by foreigners, American, British, and German (before the war, when German extraterritoriality was cancelled).

French Procedure.—Broadly speaking, judicial procedure as regards nationals is the same in the French Concession as in the International Settlement. A Britisher or an American, or any other foreigner enjoying extraterritoriality, residing in the French Concession is unquestionably under the jurisdiction of his own court in the International Settlement. The French maintain courts for their own nationals and Chinese courts function in the Concession for Chinese and foreigners who do not possess extraterritorial rights.

In the early days of the International Settlement some of the principal Consulates had their own police forces. Now, however, the policing of the foreign settlements is entirely within the hands of the Shanghai Municipal Police and the French Police, each operating exclusively within their own districts, but in cordial and efficient cooperation. The same applies to the two fire departments, and to other civic bureaux.

JURISDICTION OF NATIONALS

American Court. — The United States Court for China was created by Congress, June 30, 1906. It is composed of a judge appointed by the President for ten years, and a district attorney, marshal and clerk whose terms are at the pleasure of the President. This court sits regularly at Shanghai and is required to sit once a year in Canton, Tientsin and Hankow. Prisoners sentenced by this court are sent either to Bilibid Prison in Manila or to the United States.

British Courts. — Under the Foreign Jurisdiction Act of 1890 Great Britain established jurisdiction over British subjects in China, exercised by a Supreme Court (set up in Shanghai in 1865) and provincial courts, which cover all criminal and civil matters, including divorce. The British Court ordinarily sits at Shanghai, but can convene at any other place in China. Criminal sentences are executed in China, but there is power to send convicted persons to Hongkong to serve their sentences. Death sentences must be confirmed by H.B.M. Minister to China.

French Courts. — The Sino-French treaty of Whampoa, October 24, 1844, provides that French citizens in China are under French jurisdiction. There are seventeen French consular courts in China and judicial functions in Peiping (Peking) are performed by the Legation, according to a decree of January 31, 1881. In 1917 a judge was attached to the Shanghai consular court. There is no public prosecutor attached to the consular courts, the duties of the examining magistrate being performed by the Consul. Criminal cases may be carried to the courts of appeal at Saigon or Hanoi. As a general rule, the laws of France are administered in the French courts in China and there is no appeal from judgments in simple police cases. An appeal to the Supreme Court is brought before the Court of Cessation in Paris.

Belgium obtained extra-territorial rights in China by the treaty of Peiping (Peking), November 2, 1865. There is no permanent consular court, but a court can be formed when and if required. The administration of justice in the Belgian consular courts in China is subject to the control of the Royal Procurator General at Brussels and appeal may be made to the final court at Brussels. The Belgian Consul in China judges petty offenses and there is no appeal from his decisions. In major criminal cases defendants are sent to Brussels for trial.

Danish Consular Court. — Regulations of the Danish Court in China are based upon an act of Parliament of February 15, 1895, and all authority vests in the Danish Consular Court in Shanghai, the Consul General being the consular judge. In civil cases the Danish court of appeal is in Copenhagen and, upon demand, a criminal accused by the Danish Consul in Shanghai, may be sent to the authorities in Denmark.

Italian authorities in China have legally controlled Italian subjects since the conclusion of a treaty at Tientsin in 1866 between China and Italy. The Italian Consul General, his substitute, or his delegate, may sit as a single judge or preside over the consular court. Italian subjects living in the French Concession or the International Settlement are answerable to the respective municipal by-laws. Italians may be expelled from the consular district by consular decree if their conduct does not harmonize with public peace and order, or for moral or political reasons.

Japan Retains Rights. — By the Shimonoseki Treaty of 1896 China relinquished extra-territorial rights in Japan while Japan retained them in China. The Japanese consular official in China is empowered to hear and decide all civil and criminal cases, following the procedure of the courts of Japan. Criminal cases are sent to Japan for trial if the Minister of Foreign Affairs so instructs. Criminal sentences are served in the prison attached to the consulate or, in case of a long term, the prisoner may be sent to Japan.

The Netherlands obtained extra-territorial status for its nationals by a treaty signed at Tientsin, October 6, 1863. In civil and criminal cases the laws of The Netherlands are followed, with some minor exceptions. In commercial cases regard must be given to well established local usages of trade.

Norwegian jurisdiction follows a law of March 29, 1906, and the Norwegian Consul General at Shanghai is the consular judge. If a crime penalty exceeds three years the case must be referred to the courts in Norway and appeal lies with the Supreme Court in Oslo.

Jurisdiction over Portuguese citizens in China is provided by a treaty concluded between China and Portugal in 1887. The laws of Portugal are applied in all cases and the decision is subject to appeal to the high judicial court in Goa, Portuguese India. Criminal sentences are served by exile in Portuguese colonies in Western Africa. These cases have to be sent to the judicial court at Macao. There is no death penalty in Portuguese law.

Spanish Law Observed.—The basis of Spanish consular authority in China was established by a treaty of 1864. The Spanish consul forms the consular court and the Spanish law is followed. The Consul takes no note of offenses committed by Spanish

subjects in which no arms have been used and which have not resulted in bloodshed. In these cases the Consul proceeds officially, associating with him two Spaniards, or, failing them, two foreigners of repute.

Sweden's consular rights are based on the treaty concluded between Sweden, Norway and China on March 20, 1847. Another treaty between Sweden and China was concluded on July 2, 1908, confirming the special rights acquired by Sweden. Judicial functions are concentrated in the hands of the consular judge, the Swedish law being followed generally although local conditions are taken into consideration. Appeals are made to Stockholm.

Chapter Three
SHANGHAI'S COMMERCIAL IMPORTANCE

SHANGHAI'S geographical location made its future as a great commercial centre inevitable. Although on a tributary, it commands the commerce of the Yangtsze Kiang, listed as the third longest river in the world, streaming thirty-one hundred miles across Asia from its source in Thibet to the Pacific. It is literally the main highway of a vast empire of 700,000 square miles and more than 200,000,000 people.

Statistics alone cannot make visual the strategic position Shanghai occupies in world commerce. A glance at the map of China, however, pictures it as the cork of a vast bottle containing the major share of a great nation's vital life, the first city of the largest continent in the world. Equally distant in shipping time from Western Europe and the Eastern United States, Shanghai is an obvious centre of world commerce.

Half of China Drained. — The watershed of the Yangtsze river includes about half of China proper. The river, from Shanghai to Hankow, a distance of some 600 miles, provides a fairway of eight to ten feet of navigable depth in Winter and 28 to 30 feet in Summer. Above Hankow the river may be navigated during the Summer for another 800 miles while junks and small steamers go much farther. An area of approximately 50,000 square miles supports a population of forty million people and that area is directly adjacent to Shanghai. The city is the distributing port for more than one-tenth of the inhabitants of the entire world.

The latest available returns published by the Chinese Maritime Customs show that in 1933 the total foreign trade of China amounted to 1,957 million dollars, comprising 1,345-million for imports and 612 million for exports. Of this volume of foreign trade Shanghai's share was 54.14 per cent., representing an increase of 8.66 over the figures for the previous year.

There are six major shipbuilding concerns in Shanghai. The city owns nine drydocks. The harbour has an area of 3,230 acres with about a quarter of this area available for anchorage.

Opposite Shanghai, on the Whangpoo, is Pootung, commercially a part of Shanghai.

The number of vessels entering and sailing from the port of Shanghai during 1933, with tonnage, were as follows:

Ships	Cleared	Tonnage
Ocean and Coast liners	6,084	14,982,000
River steamers	1,789	2,539,854
Sailing vessels	414	92,680
Launches	910	57,626
Inland steamers	14,025	1,951,002
Total	**23,222**	**19,623,002**
	Entered	Tonnage
Ocean and Coast liners	5,715	14,646,494
River steamers	1,871	2,743,411
Sailing vessels	405	90,682
Launches	910	57,626
Inland steamers	14,245	2,152,596
Total	**23,112**	**19,701,687**

Industrial Development. — Less than fifty years ago the first electrically operated manufacturing plant was established in Shanghai; since then there has been a tremendous growth in the industrial wealth of the city.

It is estimated that there are now 2,709 factories in Shanghai, of which 82 are cotton mills and 124 cotton weaving plants, cotton manufactures representing one of the principal sources of Shanghai's prosperity. More than one-half of the spindles operating in China are in Shanghai.

It is worth noting that in Shanghai, one of the world's great cotton manufacturing centres, the first modern mill was established in 1889 and on May 10, 1897, the first foreign (British) mill was opened.

The total number of Chinese-owned factories is about 2,000, with an approximate gross capitalization of $300,000,000. About 250,000 workers are employed in these plants.

In addition to cotton mills other important factories are listed as follows: silk reeling, 112; silk weaving, 473; knitting, 136; silk lace, 39; flour mills, 14; rice mills, 53; cigarette factories (many of them small), 265; canned goods, 38; cosmetics, 31, candles and soap, 30; machinery, 217; hardware, 55, etc.

PUBLIC UTILITIES

Shanghai enjoys excellent public utility services, justly boasting modern installations and efficient and economical distribution to patrons.

The Shanghai Waterworks Co., Ltd., and the Shanghai Gas Co., Ltd., are owned by British interests while the Shanghai Telephone Co. and the Shanghai Power Co. are controlled by American capital.

Gas.—The organization of the Shanghai Gas Co., Ltd., the oldest but one of the most enterprising of Shanghai's public utilities, was undertaken in 1862, and gas for lighting was first produced on November 1. 1865.

At that time the price of gas was $4.50 per 1,000 cubic feet, there were 58 consumers, and five miles of mains. The price is now $2.85 per 1,000 cubic feet, and the last report showed 13,384 consumers, and 194 miles of gas mains. The entire city is served, the gas company which previously operated in the French Concession having been acquired in July, 1886.

To meet the demands for its product, the gas company in 1931 planned a new plant in the Yangtszepoo district. This plant, declared by engineers to be the most modern in the world, was opened in February, 1934. Designed to produce 4,000,000 cubic feet of gas per day, extensions to bring the production to 10,000,000 cubic feet have been provided for. The Shanghai Gas Co. manifestly have faith in the future of Shanghai.

Light and Power.— The story of the development of the Shanghai Power Co. closely parallels the story of the development of the city itself, during the past fifty years, and there is much of interest in the recital.

The old Shanghai Electric Co. was founded in 1882 and the first public display of electric light was made on July 26 of that year. The Shanghai Club first used electric light on September 25 and on November 11 the Taotai of Shanghai (chief Chinese official of the district), issued an edict forbidding Chinese to use electric light! The edict was soon smothered by public demand. Today the Chinese are perhaps the most liberal users of electric light. By June, 1883, The Bund was illuminated by electricity.

In 1893 the Shanghai Municipal Council bought the electric

Shanghai Power Company's Plant

company and owned, operated and developed it until August, 1929, when it was transferred to the present Shanghai Power Co.

The power plant of the Shanghai Power Co. in the Yangtsz-epoo district, an imposing sight on the right bank of the Whang-poo river as a steamer approaches the city, is one of the largest in the world, with a total generating capacity of about 185,000 kilowatts. The plant consumed 550,000 tons of coal in 1933.

At the first of 1934 the company was supplying power and light to 73,642 customers, an increase of 7.8 per cent. in a year. The population served is estimated at 2,225,000, as the company not only serves the International Settlement but also furnishes much of the light and power consumed in the French Concession and the Municipality of Greater Shanghai. More than 1,000 miles

of lines are in service.

Telephone Service. — Thanks to its complete reconstruction during the past few years, the plant of the Shanghai Telephone Co. gives Shanghai a service second to none elsewhere, as visitors will soon learn for themselves.

At the end of 1933 there were 49,401 telephones in service, an increase for the year of 10.75 per cent., and 92 per cent. of the subscribers were served by automatic equipment. Completed toll calls in 1933 totalled 3,211,700, an increase of 175 per cent. over 1932. Average daily calls were 504,200, an increase of 38 per cent. The average number of completed calls per subscriber per day increased more than 100 per cent. over 1931, before automatic service was installed. The company operates in both the International Settlement and the French Concession and the 1933 annual report valued the plant at Tls. 29,027,145.93.

The Shanghai Telephone Co. dates back only to 1929, when the International Telephone and Telegraph Co. took over the old Shanghai Mutual Telephone Co., formed and financed the new company, and directed the conversion to the automatic system, a tremendous task which, however, was completed in less than twenty months.

Waterworks. — The Shanghai Waterworks Co., Ltd., was incorporated in England in 1880 with a capital of £100,000. The authorized capital is now £1,164,000, Taels 2,000,000 and $3,000,000 (Mex.) and the population served is well over a million.

The company was formally opened in 1883 by the then Viceroy of the Province, His Excellency Li Hung Chang. The record of the company has since been one of constant development. The original plant was designed to supply 3,000,000 gallons per day whereas the plant now is capable of meeting a demand of over seventy million gallons.

The area served by the company is the International Settlement and roads constructed by the Shanghai Municipal Council beyond Settlement limits. An "off peak" supply is also provided for the company supplying the French Concession, while a stand-by bulk supply is given to the Chapei Waterworks. Altogether the company's distribution mains have a mileage of nearly 185. The average daily consumption in 1933 was 45,231,796 gallons.

The source of supply is the Whangpoo River, from which the water is pumped into settling tanks, and is then passed partly by gravitation or a further stage of pumping into the filtration system. The Whangpoo River is one of the most turbid and polluted sources of water supply in the World, but the standard of purity eventually obtained gives a bacterial reduction of 99.99 per cent., or a standard equal to any and superior to many in the West.

*   *   *

Shanghai in the fifties had neither gas nor, of course, electricity. Street lighting was done by means of oil lamps at a cost of $12 per month for the city.

Chapter Four
POPULATION

THE sixth largest city in the world, Shanghai, according to accurate semi-official estimates in February, 1934, had a population of 3,350,570. Indications are that Shanghai in 1935 will
rank fifth. Latest available statistics:

London	8,202,818	Berlin	4,000,000
New York	6,930,446	Chicago	3,376,438
Tokyo	5,312,000	Shanghai	3,350,570

There is, in fact, a possibility that Shanghai now ranks fifth.
Statistics compiled by officials of the City Government of Greater
Shanghai at the end of June, 1934, indicated a population for the
entire city of 3,402,748, and in this total no allowance was made
for increases during the previous few months in the International
Settlement and the French Concession, where the Chinese do not
make a monthly check as they do in their own areas. Assuming
that the Chinese authorities are correct, and they are usually accurate, it is not unreasonable to estimate that at this writing (July,
1934) Shanghai has a population in excess of 3,425,000.

Statistical Sources. — Divided as Shanghai is, into three separate municipalities, it is impossible to obtain a definitely dated,
official population total. The last official census in the International Settlement was taken in 1930; the next one will be taken
in 1935. A census was taken in the French Concession in 1932.
Statistics of the International Settlement, French Concession, and
the City Government of Greater Shanghai were used in the compilation of this chapter.

It is literally true that for the compilation of accurate, up-to-
the-minute totals of its population by racial groups, Shanghai is
growing so rapidly, the ratio of growth increasing annually, that
it is out-speeding its historians and statisticians.

1932 Computation. — Figures compiled in 1932 and published in 1933 by the Shanghai Civic Federation, based on the 1930 International Settlement census, the 1932 French Concession census, and the latest available statistics from the City Government of Greater Shanghai, were as follows:

GREATER SHANGHAI (CHINESE):
Chinese 1,571,089
Foreigners 9,347

Total 1,580,436

INTERNATIONAL SETTLEMENT:
Chinese 1,030,554
Foreigners 44,240

Total 1,074,794

FRENCH CONCESSION:
Chinese 462,342
Foreigners 16,210

Total 478,552

Total Chinese 3,063,985
Total Foreigners 69,797

Shanghai, grand total 3,133,782

It is interesting, if not convincing, to note that Professor Charles Richet, President of the French Academy of Sciences, announced in May, 1934, that his investigations showed that Shanghai's annual growth, in ratio to population, was the largest of the world's great cities. Furthermore, he estimated on a basis of fixed mathematical calculations that in 1944 the ranking by population would be as follows: New York, Tokyo, Shanghai,

Berlin, Moscow, London, and Chicago, with Osaka, Leningrad, Paris and Buenos Aires following in the order named. Territorial accretions or contractions, of course, may upset the professor's calculations.

That there is sound basis for the forecast, however, is disclosed by a brief analysis of Shanghai's growth. Population gains at first were slow. According to one authority the foreign population of the Foreign Settlement was 50 in 1844, and in 1850 the total was 175. A census of 1860 showed 569 foreigners, including 294 British, 125 Americans, 59 Indians and 91 "others." There was a "boom" in the next five years, the first municipal census of 1865 listing 2,235 foreigners, among them 1,329 British, 360 Americans and 175 Germans.

Depression followed the Taiping Rebellion and by 1870 the foreign population had decreased to 1569. A recovery to 2197 was made by 1880, and each subsequent census has shown a substantial gain.

Remarkable Growth.—The remarkable growth of modern Shanghai is revealed by the fact that twenty years ago, in 1915, the census listed 18,519 foreigners in the International Settlement and 2,405 in the French Concession, a total of 20,924, including 7,387 Japanese, 5,521 British and 1,448 Americans. At that time the total population of the city was estimated at 1,500,000. Twen-

PRINCIPAL FOREIGN GROUPS IN SHANGHAI (1930 CENSUS)

Nationality	International Settlement	External Roads Areas	French Concession	Total
Japanese	12,788	5,690	318	18,796
British	4,606	1,615	2,228	8,449
Russian	3,113	374	3,879	7,366
American	1,145	463	1,541	3,149
Indian (British)	1,758	84	—	1,842
Portuguese	847	485	267	1,599
German	524	399	507	1,430
French	159	39	1,208	1,406
Tonkinese (French)	—	—	941	941
Filipino	356	31	—	387
Danish	143	43	164	350
Polish	159	28	156	343
Italian	168	29	123	320
Spanish	116	32	73	221
Swiss	93	32	81	206
Dutch	42	40	108	190
Greek	109	12	64	185
Norwegian	84	20	69	173
Korean	139	12	—	151
Czecho-Slovakian	88	12	39	139
Austrian	64	24	44	132
Swedish	44	43	31	118
Belgian	25	2	61	88

ty years later, at this writing, Shanghai is nearing the 3,500,000 mark. In 1920 the total population was estimated at 2,000,000, a census then showing 953,375 in the International Settlement and French Concession.

Classification by Nationalities. — There are forty-eight distinct nationalities represented in Shanghai, the principal classifications being shown in the preceding table.

The total listing of foreigners in Shanghai (1930 census) follows: International Settlement, 26,965; external roads areas, 9,506; French Concession, 12,835 — Total, 48,806.

Heavy Russian Immigration. — In the past four years, of course, there have been large increases in these figures. For instance, the Russians now probably are the largest single group, due to a continued heavy immigration from Siberia and Man-

churia. The Russian population is estimated at 25,000, of whom 22,000 are actually registered. A 1932 census in the French Concession listed 6,045 Russians, an increase of more than 2,000 in two years, which practically accounted for the total increase in the foreign population of the French Concession as of 1932, which was given at 15,462 against 12,335 in 1930.

It is interesting to note that this tabulation shows the French in fourth place among foreigners in their own Concession, being outnumbered by the Russians, British, and Americans, a ratio that still exists, and that in all Shanghai in 1930 they were outnumbered by the Germans by the very close margin of 24. It is believed that the German population has increased much more than the French during the past four years.

*   *   *

So far as is known, the first white woman to come to Shanghai was Mrs. A. Lockhart, a sister of Sir Harry Parkes, British Minister to China, 1882-5. She landed here in 1843, the year Shanghai was opened to foreign trade.

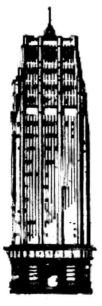

The Bund, Shanghai

Chapter Five
ARRIVAL AT SHANGHAI

THE CHINA SEA! There is romance in the very words. The other side of the world, the Orient, the Yellow Land. And just about forty miles at sea from the river even the water, which was blue a few minutes ago, becomes yellow. The mighty Yangtsze River brings down with it to the sea a great quantity of the soil of China. It is the mouth of the Yangtsze which you are entering as the pilot boards the ship at Bell Buoy some four or five hours before arrival in Shanghai. It is the pilot's task to navigate your steamer up the Yangtsze, into the Whangpoo River and to Shanghai. The Whangpoo empties into the Yangtsze at Woosung.

Shanghai is situated fifty-four miles from the mouth of the Yangtsze. It is forty miles to Woosung and fourteen miles from Woosung up the Whangpoo to Shanghai.

In the Whangpoo on both sides of the steamer are green fields and busy farm life. Junks sail by, and diminutive craft called "sampans."

In contrast, the great steamships of great nations are passing. In rapid succession it is possible to see the flags of the Scandinavian countries, Holland, Japan, Italy, England, Germany, France, America and China. Warships are always in Shanghai harbour, representing France, Japan, Italy, Great Britain, America, and occasionally, Germany; submarines, destroyers, troop carriers, battleships, cruisers, aeroplane carriers.

Passport and Customs Formalities. — The usual passport requirements and Customs formalities have to be complied with before landing in Shanghai. Have your customs declaration prepared in advance. Don't try to be evasive. Customs examiners are courteous and efficient. Tourists entering Shanghai are allowed to bring in 25 cigars, 200 cigarettes and half a pound of tobacco. Excess smoking materials are dutiable. Firearms must be deposited with the Customs until departure. Unaccompanied baggage is placed in bond until the arrival of the passenger for examination. Storage charges are thirty cents a day (Mex.) per package.

Visitors travelling overland to Shanghai by rail are, of course, subject to Customs and passport regulations at the point of entry into China.

The importation of goods into any port of China is subject to duty. Personal effects are not liable, nor are books, charts and maps, newspapers and periodicals. It is strictly prohibited to import salt, or any kind of narcotics except in certain quantities contained in medicines. Salt is a government monopoly and a great source of revenue.

Canidrome
Ballroom

•

The Rendezvous of Shanghai's Elite

OPEN ALL THE YEAR ROUND—
BALLROOM IN WINTER; LOVELY
GARDEN DURING SUMMER MONTHS

Always Something Different in Floor Shows
First-class Cuisine

•

Music by Teddy Weatherford
Presenting Buck Clayton & his Harlem Gentlemen

You must visit the CANIDROME BALLROOM

Tels. 73966
73969   J. A. ANDREW, *Manager.*

The highest duty is on woollen piece goods and silks, ranging from 80 down to 50 and 40 per cent. The next highest duty is paid on alcoholic liquor. The lowest rates are on machinery, iron tools, etc. The tariff is designed to protect and promote China's rapidly growing home industries. Export duties are very low.

In passing luggage through the Customs the assistance of one of the several reliable transport firms is helpful. Their representatives meet all passenger vessels and may be identified by the name of the firm on the cap.

Passengers should bear in mind when departing that a permit to ship, issued by the Customs, is required for all nailed cases or crates taken on board as luggage. Here again the assistance of a reliable transport firm saves a lot of trouble.

Chapter Six
SEEING SHANGHAI

SHANGHAI SYMPHONY

COSMOPOLITAN Shanghai, city of amazing paradoxes and fantastic contrasts; Shanghai the beautiful, bawdy, and gaudy; contradiction of manners and morals; a vast brilliantly-hued cycloramic, panoramic mural of the best and the worst of Orient and Occident.

Shanghai, with its modern skyscrapers, the highest buildings in the world outside of the Americas, and its straw huts shoulder high.

Modern department stores that pulse with London, Paris, and New York; native emporiums with lacquered ducks and salt eggs, and precious silks and jades, and lingerie and silver, with amazing bursts of advertising colour and more amazing bursts from advertising musicians, compensating with gusto for lack of harmony and rhythm.

Modern motors throbbing with the power of eighty horses march abreast with tattered one-man power rickshaws; velveted limousines with silk-clad Chinese multi-millionaires surrounded by Chinese and Russian bodyguards bristling with automatics for protection against the constant menace of kidnapping (foreigners are not molested); Chinese gentlemen in trousers; Chinese gentlemen in satin skirts.

Shanghai the bizarre, cinematographic presentation of humanity, its vices and virtues; the City of Blazing Night; cabarets; Russian and Chinese and Japanese complaisant "dance hostesses"; city of missions and hospitals and brothels.

Men of title and internationally notorious fugitives tip cocktails in jovial camaraderie; Colonels' Ladies and Judy O'Gradys promenade in peacock alley; social celebrities and convivial cocottes; ladies who work; ladies who shirk; ladies who live to love;

ladies who love to live.

Behold! "The longest bar in the world!"

The shortest street in the world with a blatant cacophony of carnality from a score of dance-halls; scarlet women laughing without mirth; virgins in search of life; suicides; marriages; births; carols of vested choirs; cathedral chimes; Communists plotting; Nationalism in the saddle; war in Manchuria!; it's a great old town, and how we hate it and love it!

Vital, vibrant, vivacious; strident, turbulent, glowing—Shanghai is the Big Parade of Life of every colour, race, tempo; the bitter end of the long trail for many wastrel souls; the dawn after the dark for others.

Shanghai the incomparable!

So this is Shanghai!

Let's take a look at it!

THE BUND

Let's start at The Bund, the muddy tow-path of fifty years ago which has magically become one of the most striking and beautiful civic entrances in the world, faced from the West by an impressive rampart of modern buildings and bounded on the East by the Whangpoo river. It is the natural starting point for our tour of Shanghai, for it is here that a large majority of newcomers to Shanghai first step foot in the city.

The Bund is a development of commercial necessity, not in origin the result of a calculated plan for civic improvement. In the early Land Regulations it was specified at the instance of Chinese authorities that in the building of the city a wide space should be reserved on the riverfront to preserve the tow-path used by trackers (coolies pulling boats with ropes). Shanghai's beautiful "front door" of today is the result of this precaution.

The handsome boulevard is flanked by a park space which extends to the river-edge with its unobtrusive landing stages, where tenders bring passengers from great ocean liners, most of which dock elsewhere to the North or South or make fast to anchored river buoys in midstream.

At the northern end of The Bund is the Garden Bridge, spanning Soochow Creek, which separates downtown Shanghai from the Hongkew district. Soochow Creek is colourful, teeming with small Chinese craft skillfully navigated by natives, men, women, and children, most of whom are born, live and die on the water.

The British Consulate. — At The Bund approach to the Garden Bridge is the Public Garden, a miniature but beautiful park. The large, imposing building to the left is the British Consulate. Across the bridge, to the right, are the historic Astor House Hotel, and the Russian, German and Japanese Consulates. Much of interest in shopping districts and native life is to be seen in the district north of Garden Bridge.

Retrace The Bund to Nanking Road, flanked by Sassoon House (Cathay Hotel) and the Palace Hotel. Facing the end of Nanking Road from across The Bund is a monument erected to the memory of Sir Harry Parkes, G.C.M.G., K.C.B., Envoy Extraordinary and Minister Plenipotentiary to Japan, 1865-82, and to China, 1882-5. This monument was erected "in 1890 by the foreign merchants in memory of his great services."

The Custom House. — Continue South along The Bund, business blocks to the right, the muddy Whangpoo river to the left with its constantly shifting panorama of busy commerce. Three blocks from Nanking Road is the imposing building of the Chinese Maritime Customs. The original Custom House on the same

The Garden Bridge

site was an old Chinese building, formerly a Temple. The new building is one of the finest structures in Shanghai, its lofty clock tower a striking feature of The Bund skyline. The great clock is generally referred to as "Big Ching."

Facing the Custom House is a statue and monument to Sir Robert Hart, an early Inspector General of the Chinese Maritime Customs in Shanghai (1863) and once guardian of the heir-apparent to the throne of China. Also opposite the Custom House, across The Bund, is the Customs' examination shed, flanking the pontoon for ship tenders.

Petting the Lions.—Note the huge lions guarding the entrance to the imposing building of the Hongkong and Shanghai Banking Corporation. Their paws have been polished by the caresses of millions of Chinese passers-by, who believe they derive strength from this contact with the kings of beasts. There is also a belief (unverified) among the Chinese that gold was accidentally used in the casting of the figures.

Proceed South along The Bund another block and you reach the stately canopied entrance of the Shanghai Club (British but accepting other nationals as members), widely renowned as possessing the "longest bar in the world," a distinction which has been challenged since the abolition of prohibition in the United States.

The adjoining road intersection some fifty yards farther on is the beginning of Avenue Edward VII, the boundary between the International Settlement and the French Concession and the principal traffic channel to the latter district. Facing Avenue Edward VII, on The Bund, is the Allied War Memorial erected in honour of foreign Shanghailanders who were killed in active service in the World War.

Across Avenue Edward VII is an extension of The Bund, the French Bund (Quai de France), a very active shipping and commercial centre. Here, a few steps inland from the river, is the ancient native Chinese city. More about it later.

CENTRAL DISTRICT

Foochow Road. — Retracing the way North along The Bund of the International Settlement one comes to Foochow Road, flanking the South side of the Hongkong & Shanghai Bank, and well worth a brief tour. Foochow Road, to the West, just before it terminates at Thibet Road (the Race Course), is famous as a centre of entertainment for Chinese.

Two blocks from The Bund on Foochow Road brings one to the Metropole Hotel and Hamilton House, at the Kiangse Road intersection, and in the next block, on to Honan Road, are located the new Central Police Station and the American Club, to the left, and, on the right, occupying the full block, the administration building of the Shanghai Municipal Council, housing the headquarters of the Shanghai Volunteer Corps as well as most of the chief departments of the city government.

Proceeding beyond Honan Road, still going West, one enters the very picturesque Chinese section with its gaily decorated, banner-dressed tea houses, restaurants and hotels. Several leading Chinese theatres are in the neighbourhood. Thibet Road, to the left and right, at the termination of Foochow Road, with its group of large Chinese hotels facing the Race Course, is also worth inspection.

Nanking and Bubbling Well Roads. — Nanking Road, the principal retail

The Cathay Hotel

[54]

business street of Shanghai, extends West from The Bund at Sassoon House (Cathay Hotel) and the Palace Hotel to the Race Ground and Public Recreation Ground (a magnificent public park) near the Thibet Road intersection, where Nanking Road magically and without warning becomes Bubbling Well Road, designated by an eminent American author as one of "the seven most interesting streets in the world."

Lower Nanking Road, from The Bund westward, is largely devoted to hotels, department stores, and speciality shops, practically all of them foreign-owned. Almost anything one cares to purchase in the way of foreign goods may be found in the first three blocks of Nanking Road.

Museum. — Visitors interested in the flora and fauna, sticks, stones and skeletons of China should pay a visit to the Museum of the Royal Asiatic Society, 20 Museum Road. It is situated two blocks from The Bund, along Peking Road. There are prehistoric relics of great interest and noteworthy collections of gems, coins, etc. Displays are marked with dates and Dynasties. Catalogues are on hand with complete information.

Trinity Cathedral. — One block South (to the left) of Nanking Road on Kiangse Road is the Trinity Cathedral, an historic landmark, where the first Episcopal Church in Shanghai was erected in 1847. Work on the present striking edifice was begun in 1866. Westminster chimes sound from its tower.

Continuing up Nanking Road from Kiangse Road one begins to encounter with increasing frequency the colourful Chinese shops, with their fascinating displays of silks, embroideries, linens, jewellery and other wares of Chinese manufacture, and beyond Honan Road come the large Chinese shops. These are usually vividly painted and display fluttering pennants, advertising sales and wares in large red Chinese characters. The thin wailing of Chinese music tinkles from the upper floors of these shops and everywhere is the busy clatter of Chinese commercial life. At night this section of Nanking Road is a glittering fairyland with the brilliant display of multi-coloured lights which all Chinese adore and which illuminate the lofty towers of the three largest department stores in China.

Buddhist Temple. — Between Shanse Road and Fokien Road is a Buddhist Temple, Hung Miao, one of the most popular Chinese temples in Shanghai, daily visited by hundreds. Here are shrines to Midoo and Waydoo. The chief idol, however, is that of Kwan-yin, Goddess of Mercy. To the right of the entrance passage is an enclosure with images on three sides, seventeen in the centre and twenty-three on each side. This is one of the temples in Shanghai which should be seen.

Bubbling Well Road begins at the Thibet Road intersection. It is here flanked on the left by the Race Course and Public Recreation Ground, and on the right by a number of impressive buildings, including the China United Assurance Society, which also houses a large apartment-hotel; the lofty Foreign Y.M.C.A., and the towering 22-storey building of the Joint Savings Society, containing the Park Hotel, the tallest building in the world outside of the Americas.

Up till 1862 the Settlement boundary terminated at the Race Course and the "Shanghai Riding Course" occupied the ground at the western termination of the present Nanking Road, In that year so many Chinese fled into the Settlement from the Taiping rebels that the trustees of the Shanghai Riding Course decided to construct a road 40-feet wide through the centre of the Course. This was originally intended to be a driving road only. It was completed in October, 1863, two miles to the Well. Only subscribers to the Riding Course were permitted to drive on it free and gates were erected to exclude non-subscribers.

The present race course, officially named the "Recreation

Nanking Road

Ground," is controlled by the Shanghai Race Club and the Recreation Fund Trustees. There is a swimming pool, cricket grounds, golf club, baseball field, tennis courts, rugby and football grounds, and the race track.

Proceeding, beyond Chengtu Road are located the Italian Consulate, the American Women's Club, and the Country Club, to the left, and a short distance farther, to the right, the International Recreation Club.

Intersecting a little further up Bubbling Well Road is Yates Road, otherwise known as "Petticoat Lane." Every feminine visitor to Shanghai is particularly interested in Yates Road as it is lined with shop after shop devoted to the making and displaying of silk "undies" and things of the sort.

In its further extension to the West, Bubbling Well Road is largely a residential area. This district, however, is rapidly changing in character and during recent years the section between Carter Road and Avenue Haig has expanded into an important shopping centre.

"Bubbling Well."—Bubbling Well Road derives its name

The last
round up
at the
Venus.

The Venus
Rhythm
Boys.

Shanghailanders say the

VENUS CAFE

IS THE MOST OUTSTANDING CABARET
IN TOWN

●

The Venus is located in the world-famous spot—
CHAPEI, scene of the Sino-Japanese hostilities in
1932, at the rear of the Isis Theatre
on North Szechuen Road.

●

All food is prepared in a Model Kitchen
under scrupulous conditions of cleanliness.

S. H. LEVY *is the Proprietor*
and his 10 years' experience is
always at the service of patrons.

老

大

華

舞

廳

[58]

from the famous well situated at the Avenue Haig intersection, opposite the cemetery. The Well dates back to the third century. Many fanciful legends have been woven into its history. Its action is due to the eruption of carbonic acid gas. The Bubbling Well cemetery, opposite the Well, should be visited.

Bubbling Well Temple. — To the right of the Bubbling Well itself is the famous Ching An Ssu Temple, dating back to 250 A.D. On entering, three gods, the rulers, of Heaven, Earth, and Water, may be seen. Through the door to the left is a portly Buddha. A door to the right leads to the court of the main Temple building. Buddha sits in the centre shrine on a square lotus, below him a smaller image. Grouped around the walls are life-sized intimates of Buddha in gilded wood. They are Pah-ha, with a globe in his hand; Quah Tan, with a staff; two nameless ones sitting with Koe Yun the armless; Li Kon-lan wears top boots, probably out of deference to the tiger at his feet; Long Ho bravely holds a lion in his hands; Loo Hon does nothing in particular. This Temple is well worth seeing.

Every year in the Spring a Bamboo Fair is held near this Temple. Originally the displays were articles fashioned from bamboo, but now almost any household commodity from tea pots of earthenware to dish pans of tin may be purchased at this "country fair" for amazingly low prices.

HONGKEW DISTRICT

Hongkew roughly comprises that part of the International Settlement situated north of the Soochow Creek and is best reached via the Garden Bridge or one of the bridges over the creek at Honan and Szechuen roads. As mentioned elsewhere, this quarter of the city was formerly known as the "American Settlement." In Chinese "Hongkew" means "Mouth of the Rainbow," and is derived from the fact that the shape of the boundary on the creek side resembles the arch of a rainbow.

Bordering the creek between North Szechuen Road and Broadway are a number of imposing buildings, among them being the Head Post Office, the General Hospital, a very fine institution conducted by l'Institute des Soeures Franciscaines, the Embankment Building (an apartment house), and a magnificent structure now nearing completion to be known as "Broadway Mansions."

The Temple of the Queen of Heaven. — Visitors should make a point of seeing the Temple of the Queen of Heaven, situated on North Honan Road, a few yards from the bridge. This is one of the most frequented temples in Shanghai and during festival occasions caters for enormous crowds of worshippers. In the inner court are found kiosks containing images of the gods Liu Tsiang Ching, who is credited with the ability to see anything within a distance of 333 miles of Shanghai, and Ching Tsiang Ching, who it is believed hears everything there is to hear within the same distance!

Shanse Bankers' Guild. — Along the same road, at the Boone

Head Post Office

Road intersection, will be found the Shanse Bankers' Guild, one of the most handsome structures of the kind in Shanghai. It was erected in 1892. It is an excellent example of Chinese architecture at its best. The interior decorations are extremely elaborate. Special note should be made of the carved woodwork. The guild houses a theatre with a curiously shaped dome in which it is possible to see oneself upside-down!

Hongkew Market.—A very early morning visit to this large market is recommended. It is located at the corner of Boone and Woosung Roads. Here can be seen hundreds of fishermen, farmers and butchers bringing in produce to be sold a few hours later. If it is difficult to arise at the crack of dawn it is recommended that a stop at Hongkew Market on the way to bed after a Shanghai night out is both unique and interesting. You may also purchase a live duck or lobster to take home for your "morning after" breakfast. Fruit and vegetables lie in miniature mountains to be distributed among the stalls and in huge tubs thousands of "walkee-walkee" fish (alive) gaze with indifferent eyes at the descending cleaver.

Japanese Colony.—The Japanese colony makes its home in

the area contiguous to the Hongkew market and the numerous Nipponese stores, hotels and restaurants in the neighbourhood, particularly those on Woosung and Boone Roads, have a decidedly native flair.

YANGTSZEPOO DISTRICT

The Yangtszepoo district abuts the riverfront in the Eastern part of the city and extends from Broadway along Yangtszepoo Road to the Settlement boundary at the Point. This is the most important industrial section of Shanghai. In addition to many of the principal wharves, silk and cotton mills, engineering works and warehouses, here are located the main plants of the Shanghai Power Co., one of the largest electrical undertakings in the world, the Shanghai Waterworks Co., and the Shanghai Gas Co.

THE FRENCH CONCESSION

The French Concession, like the International Settlement, abuts on the Whangpoo River which is its eastern boundary, and at the riverfront a traffic "bottle neck" is formed by the compression of the Concession between Avenue Edward VII to the North and the ancient native Chinese city to the South. As it rolls back from the river there is a lateral expansion of area. The map in this volume graphically indicates the boundaries of the French Concession, as well as other political sub-divisions.

The North side of Avenue Edward VII lies within the International Settlement, and the southern half is incorporated in the French Concession. Thus, "believe it or not," West-bound traffic on the Avenue, one of the important streets of Shanghai, is subject to French regulation while East-bound traffic is controlled by International Settlement police, the "drive to the left" rule being universal in Shanghai. The two police authorities on this Avenue, however, work in perfect harmony.

Weather Signals.—On the French Bund (Quai de France) a step South of Avenue Edward VII, is the signal tower from which are displayed the weather forecasts for the China coast as they are signalled from the world-famous Siccawei Observatory, conducted by scientists of the French Jesuits.

South on the French Bund from Avenue Edward VII, the next street is Rue du Consulat, named for the French Consulate-General, located at its intersection with the French Bund.

Rue du Consulat is well worth visiting, being lined with typical Chinese shops for several blocks. A short swing to the left then brings one from Rue du Consulat into Avenue Joffre, the principal business street of the French Concession. Here Russian merchants predominate and the Chinese advertising pennants of Rue du Consulat yield to neat Russian characters, advertising a wide variety of wares.

Russian Colony.—The Avenue Joffre section is colloquially known as "Little Russia." for it is here that the thousands of Russians who have settled in Shanghai centre their commercial and domestic lives. There is tragic romance in the story of the Russians' peaceful invasion of Shanghai. Up to 1918, there were few Russians in Shanghai. The Russian Revolution and its political and economic results put thousands of "White Russians" to flight

to the South. The Russian population of Shanghai is now approximately 25,000.

Most of them arrived in a condition of utmost destitution after battling and starving their way out of Russia and Siberia. Most of them had a desperate fight for preservation; many perished. The Russian colony in Shanghai is now, generally speaking, soundly established although there is much poverty among them. They are, on the whole, law-abiding and worthy residents.

One interesting outgrowth of their struggle for existence in a strange land is the fact that Russian girls, many of them extremely beautiful, have almost monopolized the "dancing hostess" profession in the cabarets which have added much to the colour of Shanghai's fantastic night life.

Residential District. — West from the Avenue du Roi Albert intersection with Avenue Joffre there are many beautiful homes

Hongkong & Shanghai Bank and Customs House

and gardens. This section of Avenue Joffre is almost exclusively residential. Many wealthy Russians, Chinese, French, Germans, Americans and British have built mansions in this district.

The bi-settlement Avenue Edward VII extends westward from the Bund to Avenue Foch. It is almost entirely devoted to business, both foreign and Chinese.

Generally speaking, the major business and financial activities of Shanghai are centered in the International Settlement, while the French Concession, outside of its sectional retail business districts, such as those on Avenue Joffre, is largely residential in character.

Chapter Seven
NATIVE CHINESE LIFE

IN the International Settlement Chinese social life centres in the area West of Honan Road, particularly on Foochow Road. Every visitor, of course, will want a Chinese feast and attempt the manipulation of chopsticks. It should be known that Chinese "chow" differs greatly according to the Province in which the chef was born. Cantonese food is generally agreed by foreigners to be the best, but opinions vary. Peking food is very popular, while natives of Foochow will attest that all food except in Foochow style is fit only for pigs. On Foochow Road, at any rate, there are Chinese restaurants of every type, offering Cantonese food, Ningpo banquets, Peking feasts and any other variety. There are also many Chinese tea houses on this street.

Chinese Theatres.—The Chinese theatre is another institution of interest. Judged by foreign standards, old-style Chinese stage performances on first acquaintance appear to be primitive in both form and execution.  The absence of scenery and properties, the mingling of actors, musicians, and attendants on the stage, the acrobatics, trappings and gaudy make-up of performers, are apt to bring a smile to those who do not understand the ancient traditions of the Chinese drama. The Chinese, however, concern themselves with the story being told. Every movement, every gesture, has a definite meaning and value. Inability to separate essentials from non-essentials merely shows a lack of true dramatic understanding.

Most of the old-style dramas are based on episodes in Chinese history and have been handed down from Yuan and Ming times. At present, probably as the result of the influence of the foreign "movies," the Chinese theatre shows a marked tendency to shed its old conventions. Modern plays with women taking part (a thing unheard of a few years ago) and stage "settings" in the approved Western style are frequently performed in Shanghai and other Treaty Ports and prove very popular.

There are three principal Chinese theatres in Shanghai where legitimate plays may be seen, The Tien Che, at Foochow and Honan Roads; the San Sing, on Chekiang Road near Peking Road, and the Kwong Theatre, on Avenue Edward VII near Thibet Road. There are also many Chinese cinemas (both sound and silent) in Shanghai, which should be seen to appreciate just how far the Chinese are progressing in this art. The Central Theatre on Yunnan Road and the Kwong Wha cinema on Avenue Foch, are popular Chinese cinemas as is the Kiu Sing, also on Avenue Foch. From time to time, Chinese pictures (with English sub-captions) are shown in the foreign cinema houses. In all the Chinese theatres "refreshments" are supplied together with hot towels for cleansing the face and hands.

THE CHINESE BUND

Shanghai is not China. It is everything else under the sun, and, in population at least, is mostly Chinese, but it is not the real China. For glimpses of genuine native life one must wander into the highways and byways beyond the confines of the International Settlement and French Concession.

Let's tour the Chinese Bund. It begins at the southern end of The Bund and the French Bund (Quai de France). (*See* previous chapters on The Bund and French Concession.) Begin this tour anywhere on The Bund or French Bund and continue to the South. A Chinese guide (travel agencies and hotels provide them) will be helpful.

Wood Merchants' Guild. — The Chinese Bund is one of the busiest streets in Greater Shanghai. It is part of a district known as N'antao (Southern Market). Spread along the waterfront are dockyards, hospitals, and numerous shipping, timber, and rice offices. A quarter of a mile along the Chinese Bund brings one to what appears to be a Temple. It isn't. It is the guild-house of the wood merchants from Chuchou, in the Province of Chekiang. It may be entered by a narrow lane to the left of the building. There are two open courts, a theatre, a temple. The temple houses three gods, the principal one being Lupai, to whom the wood merchants refer for the settlement of any disputes that may arise among them.

A little farther on there is an archway in a white-washed wall, opening on a square enclosed by high walls. In it is a fair and a small market, with story-tellers, peep-shows, etc.

There Goes the Bride!

Proceeding, one finds among squalid tenements one of the most magnificent guild-houses in Shanghai, the Mosang Way Kway, also a timber merchants' guild. Excellent examples of work in Chinese style are to be found in this guild with its red and gold temple and theatre, pewter storks and incense-burners, and chequered patterned walls.

Cathedral of Tungkadoo. — The Cathedral of Tungkadoo will be the next object of interest. It is a great church found in a fairly broad Chinese thoroughfare, built by Bishop de Besco, the foundation stone being laid in 1849. It is a large edifice in the classic style, white walled. There is a fine organ in the gallery.

The Chinese Bund was built in 1894, after a fire which destroyed 500 old Chinese houses. An enormous number of boats of every description line the river front. This floating population of China is permanent; the Chinese are born, live and die, on their boats.

Beyond the water tower is a splendid Cantonese guild-house with white walls, the Jau Way Way Kway. It has a clean, flagged court and a five-storey pagoda-like building at the northwest corner. Two large flower vases are carved in high relief on the walls.

THE CHINESE CITY

The Chinese Bund being, in part, the Whangpoo riverfront boundary of the Chinese City, perhaps it should next be explored. Again, a native guide is recommended. If the Chinese City tour is to be a separate one, it is best entered from the South end of Rue Montauban, through the North Gate, a one-time entrance to the old walled city.

The First Temple.—Once inside the Chinese City the first Temple may be seen. This is the Tsung Woo Day. Upstairs is an oblong apartment containing an image of Emperor Ye Fung, who was on the throne when the Temple was erected. On his left is a shrine to Kwangti, the God of War, and on his right a shrine to the Taoist trinity, the Three Pure Ones. From this Temple a long, straight street, leads to the centre of the city. Sidewalk shops containing ivory, sandalwood and fans line the street. These may be seen in the process of manufacture. There are shops for brassware, pewter, silks and porcelains. In the summer the street is canopied with blue cloth and gives the effect of a bazaar.

A turn to the left at the end of this street and then to the right (don't worry, your guide will take you there anyway) and you reach the famous Willow Pattern Tea House (Woo Sing Ding), supposed to be the original of the tea house on "willow pattern" plates. Here also are two Chinese gardens, the City Temple and smaller shrines.

The tea house is built on stone pillars in a pool, approached by zigzag bridges. Around the pool may be had a kaleidoscopic glimpse of Chinese life. Dentists, doctors, toy vendors, cooks and jugglers carry on their trades in the open with admiring spectators freely offering advice. Near the pool are several bird markets with gorgeous collections.

The City Temple is situated in the centre of a maze of crowded, narrow streets lined with every kind of shop one can imagine. The Temple is entered either by the Great East Gate or the Temple of the Three Emperors. In the Temple there is a large central court which becomes a fair almost every afternoon, largely devoted to amusement. There are refreshment stalls, incense shops, toy salesmen and jugglers who perform marvellous disappearing acts and sleight-of-hand tricks. The Temple was originally established in the Han dynasty (B.C. 206-A.D. 25) under the name "Kin Shan Liao" (Golden Hill Temple) in memory of a beloved statesman, Hou Kwang. It acquired its present name (Chan Kwang Miao) during the Ming dynasty (A.D. 1368-1644) and was rededicated to Tsing Wu Pai, a high official of the period.

The Confucian Temple. — The Confucian Temple is reached by streets largely devoted to the sale of clothing. Outside this Temple is a three-storey pagoda and facing it a pond and wall to exclude evil spirits. Along the walls of the court are sheds containing tablets to the 3,000 disciples of Confucius, the larger ones dedicated to his 70 superior disciples. Severe simplicity marks the interior of the Temple and the Tablet of Confucius holds the place of honour.

The Mandarin's Garden, nearby, is enclosed by one of the finest dragon walls in China and the Garden itself is on a miniature scale with diminutive bridges and fountains, pools and rocks.

Seekers for curios are warned that many of those to be found in the Chinese City are excellent imitations of the authentic article.

In the Chinese City the streets are named for the wares in which they specialize, such as Jade Street, Ivory Street, Bird Street, Brass Street, etc. These names, naturally, are not in English but in Chinese; consult your guide.

The Big Bad General. — A short distance from the North Gate, at the end of Rue Montauban, is Da Ching, once a guard-house or castle, now a Temple. It is a very beautiful and picturesque building, gardens surround it, and at one corner there is a pool. Youngsters may burst into lusty howls at the sight of General Chow, a black-faced warrior, who has been on guard in a narrow passage since 1100 B.C. In the hall beyond this passage is a shrine containing the figure of a famous Taoist priest and to his right is a shrine to the King of Snakes. Not a good place to go, with shaky nerves.

The main Temple area is on the second floor. Kwangti, the God of War, holds the place of honour with two gentlemen attendants. On the right is the God of Medicine, Li Zung Yang, one of the eight immortals. On the left of the God of War is Zung Wong, the protective deity of the city. At the left of the entrance is the groom and charger of the God of War; on the right his boatmen and boat. Another room has a small shrine and beautiful stained glass windows. On the top floor are three gilt figures of the Taoist trinity, the Three Pure Ones.

Ancient Figures. — In many market gardens of the Chinese City are huge ancient stone figures of horses, men, turtles, lions, much of the same type as those of the Ming tombs at Nanking. Just before reaching the South Gate, flanking which is a flourishing American mission, is the Tsi Ying An, a Temple to the Goddess of Mercy. A little farther on is the Dien Zung, the Temple of the God of Earth.

Ta Vung Leu, an old castle which has been converted into a Temple, is between the East and North gates near the city watertower. Along the passage are mural paintings of the Buddhist Hades. In the Temple are shrines to the Kitchen God. His image is in every home and the Chinese explode many fire crackers and bombs near New Year's when this God ascends to Heaven to make a detailed report of all family sins during the year. By this din they hope to placate his austere majesty so that his memory will be at fault as he makes his report. The God's lips are also smeared with sugar to further sweeten his words.

CHAPEI

Chapei, the principal district of the Chinese-governed Municipality of Greater Shanghai (refer to map), is chiefly important as an industrial section. Here is the North Railway Station (lines to Nanking and Woosung) upon which was centered the Japanese attack in the fighting early in 1932. Much of Chapei was destroyed in this undeclared war. Rapidly being rebuilt, many scars of warfare and fire yet remain in Chapei.

Chapei has many factories. Here are the famous silk filatures from which come bolts of beautiful brocaded silk.

SICCAWEI AND LUNGHUA

A visit should be made to Siccawei, a large Jesuit settlement, and Lunghua, where the only pagoda in the vicinity of Shanghai can be seen. Both places can be reached by a short motor trip via the French Concession.

Siccawei.—Siccawei has an important place in the history of Shanghai on account of its association with Hsu Kwang-ch'i, friend and pupil of Matteo Ricci, the Jesuit Missionary. Hsu was born at Siccawei in 1562, and it was from his family the Jesuits acquired their present property in the village, which since 1848 has been a centre of Roman Catholic mission work.

Among the features of the settlement are a Meteorological Observatory, a museum, industrial schools, and orphanages for boys and girls. Various handicrafts are taught in the schools and workshops, from which come beautiful examples of carved wood furniture, lace and embroidery, printing, and metal and stained glass work.

The Observatory has achieved world-wide fame as a result of its researches. It is linked up with a network of seventy stations spread over a zone that includes Irkutsk at the northwest extremity, Nemura (Japan) in the northeast, Cap St. Jacques (Indo-China) in the southwest, and Guam in the southeast. By keeping track of typhoon and storm centres, and giving advance warning of their approach, the Observatory has contributed immensely to the safety of navigation on the China coast. The Observatory also

City Hall, Civic Centre, Kiangwan

maintains an astronomical station at Zo-se and a seismological station at Lo-ka-pang.

Lunghua. — The chief attraction at Lunghua, a short distance from Siccawei, is the pagoda, which is in an excellent state of preservation. Legend dates it back to the third century. There is good reason to believe, however, that it was not built earlier than the ninth century. The pagoda may be ascended and the summit affords a fine view of the surrounding district.

Pagodas were first built in China about the third century and are Indian in origin. There are, it has been estimated, about 2,000 of them in China. They are always built with an odd number of storeys — generally seven, nine, eleven, or thirteen — in accordance with a Buddhist belief that odd numbers are lucky. The Lunghua pagoda has seven storeys.

At the East side of the Lunghua pagoda is the Temple of the King of Heaven, which should also be seen.

Time permitting, the return trip to Shanghai can be made via Chung San Road, Hungjao Road, Monument Road and Pearce Road to the Soochow Creek boundary, from which the journey is continued along Brenan Road, Yu Yuen Road and Bubbling Well Road to town. The Hungjao Road section takes in the S.M.C. Nurseries, the Hungjao Golf Links and the Aerodrome. Jessfield Park is passed at the Brenan Road and Yu Yuen Road intersection.

WOOSUNG

A trip to Woosung on one of the well-appointed ferry-boats of the City Government of Shanghai affords a good close-up view of life on the Whangpoo. Boats run at frequent intervals from Pontoon No. 13 on the Bund, opposite Nanking Road. Calls are made at Ching-ning-hsih, Tungkou, and Kaochow, where the journey can be broken. The City Government maintains an interesting experimental garden at Tungkou. Visitors are welcomed. Good hiking along the waterfront and in the country can be obtained at Kaochow. To the East of Kaochow is an excellent bathing beach, reached by bus. Meals and accommodation are available at the Beach Hotel.

Woosung village and the Forts in the neighbourhood were almost wiped out as a result of bombardment during the Sino-Japanese conflict in 1932, and although rehabilitation is taking place, many evidences of the trouble remain.

The trip to Woosung may also be made by an excellent motor highway via Kiangwan or Yangtszepoo.

Pootung.—Pootung lies across the Whangpoo from Shang-

---

hai. Much of this area, formerly marsh land, is now occupied by factories of the British-American Tobacco Co., the Japan-China Cotton Spinning and Weaving Co., several egg factories, ship yards, landing piers of various steamship companies, godowns and the warehouses of the Standard Oil Co., the Asiatic Petroleum Co., and various other concerns.

Few visitors to Shanghai, because of the vast distances usually travelled in coming here, now bring their own motor cars for pleasure tours, but some do and, of course, hire cars may be chartered here through reliable agencies for country motor trips.

Visitors who wish to land automobiles in Shanghai for a brief period may avoid paying import duty by depositing with the Chinese Maritime Customs a sum sufficient to cover duty and dues, to be returned provided the automobile is re-exported within two months. Local licenses must be obtained through the usual official channels. An International Settlement or French Concession license will serve in both districts, but an additional license must be obtained from the City Government of Greater Shanghai (Chinese) if the car is to enter Chinese territory.

Because of the first-hand, close-up view afforded of native life in the country, several short motor tours out of Shanghai are recommended.

Shanghai-Woosung Road (Woosung is 15 miles, by road,

Junks

from Shanghai, and is situated at the junction of the Yangtsze and Whangpoo rivers): Start from the North end of Yangtszepoo Road; the road closely follows the Whangpoo to the historic Woosung Forts; continuing past the Forts, turn West just before reaching Paoshan, a walled city, and a further drive brings one to the Shanghai-Liuhu Road at Liuhang, where a turn to the left will continue the journey back to Shanghai. Several other roads lead off the Woosung Road to Kiangwan and other places.

Shanghai-Liuhu Road (Liuhu is 27 miles from Shanghai): Cross the Markham Road bridge and continue to Kung Ho Road, turn right and cross the railway along Kung Ho Hsin Road, thence continuing straight on to Liuhu. By turning East at Liuhang the return to Shanghai may be made by the Woosung Road (*see* foregoing paragraph).

Chungshan Road: Start from Lunghua and make a full circuit of Greater Shanghai, from the Whangpoo river South of the city to the Whangpoo North of the city, following the route of the Shanghai-Hangchow railway through Zikawei (Siccawei), across the Shanghai Municipal Council extra-Settlement roads to the Shanghai-Nanking railway, thence passing through Chapei, back of Hongkew Park, to the Woosung Road, where a turn to the right brings one back into the city.

Shanghai-Minghong Road (Minghong is 18 miles from Shanghai): Start from Route de Zikawei by crossing the Route Ghisi bridge or Zikawei bridge, in either case turning to the right; the Chungshan Road and Shanghai-Hangchow railway are crossed shortly; continue to Minghong village, the Whangpoo river being just beyond.

By crossing the Whangpoo by the Minghong ferry, a motor tour may be made over a new road to Hangchow, 134 miles from Shanghai (*see* Chapter Twelve, "Excursions From Shanghai").

Once in Hangchow, the motorist may drive on to Nanking, 215 miles from Hangchow, through a beautiful country.

Sungkiang.—On the drive to Minghong the tourist, by turning to the right at Peichiao, 12 miles from Shanghai, will reach Sungkiang, 26 miles from Shanghai, where the tomb of General Frederick Townsend Ward, the American hero of the Taiping Rebellion, is located (*see* Chapter One, "Historical Background," for references to Ward).

NATIVE FESTIVALS

Lest the visitor to Shanghai be suddenly startled by an apparently meaningless display of fireworks, it is well to know the approximate dates of the principal Chinese festivals.

Chinese New Year.—Chinese New Year generally falls in February, that month being the Chinese first moon. Practically all native business in China during a two-week period at Chinese New Year is at a standstill, but the temples, theatres, and eating houses are thronged. On the morning of New Year's Day Chinese coolies distribute visiting cards, all the Chinese turn out in their most gorgeous attire and Nanking Road and Avenue Edward VII are so crowded that they are practically impassable. Throughout the nights there is an incessant sound of firecrackers. It is at New Year that the Chinese must meet all his financial obligations or suffer disgrace.

Feast of Lanterns.—The fifteenth day of February (first moon) is a fixed feast day. At this time the Ningpo Guild is decidedly worth a visit, at Boulevard des Deux Republiques, French Concession. It is gorgeous with lanterns.

Feast of Tsing Ming.—The Feast of Tsing Ming is a movable Chinese festival which may occur anytime from the end of March to the middle of April. It is one of the three principal festivals of China. Literally, it is the "Feast of the Dead." Practically all Chinese then worship and offer sacrifices at the graves of their ancestors. Originally it was a memorial day but it has developed into a rite to conciliate the spirits of ancestors and to retain their good favour. The Chinese, if away from home, endeavour to return to celebrate this feast.

Dai Wong Festival. — The Dai Wong festival takes place in the middle of April. A great procession starts from the Dai Wong Temple on Sinza Road about 9 a.m. An image of Dai Wong, paper flowers, immense paper dragons, banners, etc., are carried. Paper "food" is taken for offerings. Those in the procession are usually gorgeously dressed in silks and satin brocades. Eight of the fattest men form one group, dressed in splendid crimson silks. Dai Wong is the God of Rain and the guardian of the farmers.

Dragon Boat Festival. — Since its origin in 450 B.C. the Dragon Boat Festival has always taken place about the middle of June. The festival is the anniversary of a hero's death. A faithful minister of state was dismissed by his prince and threw himself into a small river in Hunan to show his humiliation. Friends, afraid that fishes would devour his body, set out to recover his corpse. They threw rice into the river so that his spirit wouldn't starve. Since then, on the anniversary of the hero's death, dragon boats race on the rivers of China, presumably looking for his body. The boats are decorated with silk hangings, banners, lamps, embroideries, etc.

Mid-Autumn Festival. — The Chung-Chin-chieh, or Mid-Autumn Festival, is in the eighth moon, about the middle of August. This occurs at full moon and altars covered with fruits may be seen in large numbers at all the Chinese shops, on the verandahs, and out in the open. Moon-cakes are eaten at this time and they may be found in red packets in all the native confectioners' shops.

FEMININE FASHIONS

To the foreign eye it would appear that Chinese ladies once found a certain style of dress, liked it, and decided to keep it forever. That is entirely wrong. Chinese styles change just as often as Occidental styles.

As in great Occidental style centres it is the men who inaugurate the season's fashions and the tailors in Shanghai set the mode for feminine dress all over China. Occidental fashions are always taken into consideration. In colour and length the prevailing foreign style is usually followed, but the skirt slits, collars and sleeves are made up according to Oriental trends and convenience. Slits, all evidence to the contrary, are not the result of a lack of modesty but simply a desire to turn masculine. High slits in Chinese men's gowns prevail and consequently the women who desire the "new freedom" also go in for high slits. At the moment slits are on the downward trend and it is becoming the Chinese mode to be feminine again.

The collar on a Chinese dress always has been and, presumably, always will be. The width of the collar, however, varies according to the length of the skirt. Sleeves, at the moment, are usually very tight. A few years ago they were extremely wide.

Material, however, stays more or less constant in China. Velvet may be decreed in Paris but silk is cheap in Shanghai and silk it remains. But the decorations of the gown change each season. They are usually selected with an eye to design and colour of the material. Simple band trimmings prevail some seasons. Lace is all the vogue during other seasons. Sometimes double band trimmings make single band trimmings old-fashioned.

Long gowns have been in fashion only for about eight years, a style taken over from the Manchus. Before that skirts and short blouses were worn by women. Girls wore trousers. After they were married they graduated to skirts but not before. Trousers were the prerogative of children and maidens. In former days women's clothing was amply padded, but today the fad for slenderness has eliminated all surplus material.

*   *   *

According to the National Health Administration of Nanking something like 6,000,000 persons in China die every year from causes other than natural ones.

Shanghai by Night

Chapter Eight
ENTERTAINMENT

NIGHT LIFE

W HOOPEE!

What odds whether Shanghai is the Paris of the East or Paris the Shanghai of the Occident?

Shanghai has its own distinctive night life, and what a life!

Dog races and cabarets, hai-alai and cabarets, formal tea and dinner dances and cabarets, the sophisticated and cosmopolitan French Club and cabarets, the dignified and formal Country Club and cabarets, prize fights and cabarets, amateur dramatics and cabarets, treatres and cabarets, movies and cabarets, and cabarets — everywhere, in both extremities of Frenchtown (French Concession), uptown and downtown in the International Settlement, in Hongkew, and out of bounds in Chinese territory, are cabarets.

AMBASSADOR
BALLROOM

●

*100 of the prettiest Dancing Hostesses
in all Shanghai for your entertainment*

●

SUPERB DANCE MUSIC GOOD
FOOD AND PURE LIQUORS

●

*Shanghai's boasted Night
Life is at its gayest at the*

AMBASSADOR
745 AVENUE EDWARD SEVENTH
Telephone No. 81381

Hundreds of 'em!

High hats and low necks; long tails and short knickers; inebriates and slumming puritans.

Wine, women and song.

Whoopee!

Let's go places and do things!

When the sun goes in and the lights come out Shanghai becomes another city, the City of Blazing Night, a night life Haroun-al-Raschid never knew, with tales Scheherezade never told the uxoricidal Sultan Shahriyar.

Tea and Cocktails. — Night life in Shanghai begins with the tea-cocktail hour, tea for propriety, cocktails for pep; it ends at anytime from 2 a.m. until breakfast. You can take your fun where you find it, and one needn't look far. The hotel clerk will tell you, or your partner in a cocktail twosome.

Formal tea and dinner dances, with elaborate entertainment, are featured by the leading hotels and the larger cabarets and ballrooms.

The cabarets — maybe we mentioned them before — are in three classifications; high class, low class and no class. You take your choice. The Number One places will be thickly dotted with dinner jackets and Paris frocks and you bring your own girl or engage in a little social piracy; the Number Two's supply the "dancing hostesses" at a moderate fee if one is stagging it, and the Number Three's — but why bring that up?

Food and Liquor. — Good food can be found everywhere, at any hour; good liquor is the pride and boast of the first class resorts—at the others stick to bottled beer, and open the bottles yourself. The entertainment is variegated, a Hawaiian hula, Russian mazurka, Parisian apache, negro musicians, dusky crooners and torch singers, Siberian acrobats, London ballroom exhibitionists, American jazz, the Carioca, the tango, and the "dancing hostesses." Ah!

Keep moving, if there is but one night; start at the hotel and finish at "Blood Alley," playground of the navies and armies. There's plenty to see and do in between.

Dancing and Music.—Shanghai flames with millions of flashing jewels at midnight. The centre of night life is a vast crucible of electric flame.

The throb of the jungle tom-tom; the symphony of lust; the music of a hundred orchestras; the shuffling of feet; the swaying of bodies; the rhythm of abandon; the hot smoke of desire—desire under the floodlights; it's all fun; it's life.

Joy, gin, and jazz. There's nothing puritanical about Shanghai.

The "dancing hostesses"—they amiably entertain at a dime to a dollar a dance; Russians, Chinese, Japanese, Koreans, Eurasians—occasionally others.

They can dance—and drink.

"Vun small bottle of vine?" It's the battle cry of the far flung bottle front.

" 'S'funny how a little girl can hold so much champagne!"

It's not wine; it's cider or ginger ale, but not on the chit (bill). Shura or Vera or Valia gets a commission. It all helps. Give this little girl a great big bottle.

" 'S getting late." Rose tints the sky beyond the Whangpoo. "Let's go for ham'n eggs and one last round."

One swaying, sinuous embrace and a moist kiss with the last strains of the dance. "Hey, kid; why don't you marry the girl?"

The modish matron cuffs the gigolo. The dancing girl nods surrender but grabs her stack of dance tickets and flees into the night.

"Boy! Call a car!"

Whoopee!

One night in Shanghai is ended.

CABARETS — BALLROOMS

Shanghai likes to dance and to be entertained. The Cathay Hotel features tea dances and dinner dances, with elaborate floor shows. During the Winter season the Astor House Hotel's tea dances and classical concerts are popular. The Palace Hotel offers concerts during the tea and dinner hours.

Of cabarets there is a range to suit any taste, from those where formal dress predominates, to those not so formal but distinctly bohemian.

Among the cabarets which may safely be recommended, because of the high standard of management and service, a tour of which will give the visitor a reasonably complete survey of Shanghai's night life, are:

Ambassador	741 Avenue Edward VII
Canidrome	1189 Rue Lafayette
Ladow's Casanova	545 Ave. Edward VII
Majestic Cafe	254 Bubbling Well Road
Palais Cafe	57 Avenue Edward VII
St. Anna Ballroom	80 Love Lane
Venus Cafe	North Szechuen Road
Vienna Ballroom	Bubbling Well Road

LOTTERY

"Invest $10 and win $500,000," the advertisements say, and it is possible.

In fact, in Shanghai, sudden and unearned wealth, like prosperity, is just "around the corner" — for the lucky ones.

In this instance the opportunity is offered by the National State Lottery Administration (Chinese Government). Drawings at this writing (July, 1934) are held every two months, with

500,000 tickets offered for sale at $10 each, each ticket in turn being divided into ten shares, at $1 a share. That is, you may have one full $10 ticket or a tenth interest in one ticket for $1. Prizes approximate $2,500,000, the net realization going into a fund for the development of highways and airways in China. Drawings are supervised by a commission composed of foreigners and Chinese. Tickets for this lottery are continuously on sale in Shanghai.

Fortunes in Prizes. — The capital prize is $500,000. If you have the full ticket for the winning number you win $500,000; if you have a tenth interest in it you win $50,000. There are two second prizes of $100,000 each, four third prizes of $50,000 each; ten fourth prizes of $10,000, fifty of $2,000, one hundred of $500, five hundred of $200, and, on terminal numbers, 4,999 prizes of $70, and 44,999 of $20.

So, if Lady Luck smiles, $10 may bring you $500,000; $1 may win $50,000. The odds are long, but — the prizes are won, and promptly paid.

Racing. — Racing in Shanghai is promoted by the Shanghai Race Club, International Recreation Club, and the Chinese Jockey Club. The magnificent new club house of the Shanghai Race Club is at the Recreation Ground, at the junction of Nanking and Bubbling Well Roads. The International Recreation Club oper-

Shooting Craps?

ates at Kiangwan. North of Shanghai, beyond Hongkew Park, and the Chinese Jockey Club's course lies beyond Yangtszepoo.

Horse racing (or rather "China pony" racing, the ponies being imported from the Mongolian plains) is practically a year 'round diversion in Shanghai. The Shanghai Race Club starts off with the New Year Race Meeting on January 1. In December the Chinese Jockey Club finishes the racing year with the "China Gold Vase" meet.

The first weeks in May and November (Saturday to Saturday, inclusive) bring the Spring and Autumn Race Meets of the Shanghai Race Club, the most important events in the racing calendar. "Champions' Day" (Wednesday) of these weeks brings for award the biggest sweepstakes of the racing year. The lucky holder of the ticket on the winning pony in these events will profit by from $70,000 to $125,000. There are many lesser sweepstakes, and most of the Shanghai social clubs conduct their own sweeps on the major events, with first prizes ranging from $2,500 to $10,000.

Wagering Systems. — Betting at the horse races is both by sweepstake and pari-mutuel methods. The International Recreation Club varies from the pari-mutuel system by employing the "totalizator" method, which is a machine instead of a manual system and by which the bettor can see at a glance how many tickets have been sold on any one pony.

In the big sweepstakes all revenue from the sale of tickets is available for prizes after the deduction of 20 per cent. of the total pool for the club. Holders of tickets on unplaced ponies are alloted ten per cent. of the prize money. The residue is divided 70 per cent. to the winning pony, twenty per cent. to the second and ten per cent. to the third. As may be imagined, the running of the

"Champions" Day at the Races

sweepstake races are among the major sporting and social events in Shanghai.

Dogs and Hai-alai. — "Going to the dogs" is literally a favourite diversion of Shanghailanders, the greyhounds racing on stated dates at the Champs de Courses Francais (Canidrome), Avenue du Roi Albert and Rue Lafayette, in the French Concession. Dog racing is not allowed in the International Settlement, and the importation of greyhounds has been prohibited by the Chinese Government, but the sport flourishes at the Canidrome in the French Concession, where greyhounds are bred, and, like pony racing, offers ample opportunity to those who would woo fickle fortune. By various combinations, big winnings, or big losings, are possible.

Hai-alai, fast and fascinating Spanish indoor sport, is a nightly feature of Shanghai sporting life, staged at the palatial Auditorium, on Avenue du Roi Albert, just off Avenue Joffre, in the French Concession. There is a huge amount of betting on the games.

THEATRES

For its theatrical entertainment Shanghai is largely dependent on motion pictures and there are a number of first class cinema houses showing the best of the American, British, German, French and Chinese productions. They are all equipped for sound.

Excellent stage plays are produced at frequent intervals by local associations of amateurs, and touring companies are occasionally here for limited engagements. But in the main going to the theatre in Shanghai means going to the "talkies."

Among the first class cinemas are:

Carlton	2 Park Road
Cathay	868 Avenue Joffre
Embassy	742 Bubbling Well Road
Grand	216 Bubbling Well Road
Lyceum	Rtes. Bourgeat and Cardinal Mercier
Metropol	500 Thibet Road
Nanking	523 Avenue Edward VII
Strand	586 Ningpo Road

Municipal Orchestra. — The Shanghai Municipal Symphony Orchestra is perhaps the chief cultural asset of the city. Under the direction of Maestro Mario Paci, conductor, the orchestra has achieved an international reputation. The personnel is made up of 44 players of various nationalities — Italian, German, Austrian, Russian, Hungarian and Czecho-Slovakian. Many notable visiting artists have collaborated with the orchestra from time to time, including Zimbalist, Moiseiwitsch, Elman, Godowsky, and McCormack.

During the Winter season the orchestra performs every Sunday evening in the Grand Theatre. These concerts are interspersed with mid-week radio broadcasts. In the Summer months band and symphony orchestra concerts are given in the public parks.

Radio Broadcasting. — Although radio broadcasts are a comparatively recent development in Shanghai, there are now more than 100 stations operating in the city, the bulk of them being Chinese. Among the principal foreign stations are the following:

Call Letters	Operated by	Metres	Kc.
XQHA	Radio Shanghai, 80 Love Lane	517.2	580
XMHA	Radio Engineering Co., 445 Race Course Road	500	600
XMHC	Radio Sales and Service Ltd., 47 Ningpo Road	428.57	700
XQHB	Mrs. C. M. Robertson, 274 Rte. Maresca	861.2	830
XQHC	China Broadcast, 269 Broadway	280.6	1300

Radio Minded.—Ninety per cent. of all radio sets sold in Shanghai go to Chinese and a large proportion of radio advertising is placed with the Chinese broadcasting stations.

HOTELS AND APARTMENTS

Shanghai offers ample hotel and hotel-apartment accommodations, with a wide variety of locations and tariffs. Customarily the American plan (meals included) prevails, but the European plan is optional at reduced rates; monthly rates are reasonable. The more modern hotels offer all the attractions and facilities obtainable elsewhere in great cities.

Principal hotels, locations and minimum American plan rates (quoted in Mexican dollars):

Astor House Hotel; 7 Whangpoo Road, immediately North of Garden Bridge; single, $12; double, $20, suite for two, $30.

Beach Hotel (Kaochow); on Whangpoo river excursion; American plan; rates on application.

Burlington Hotel; 1225 Bubbling Well Road; single $8; double, $15.

Cathay Hotel (Sassoon House); The Bund and Nanking Road; European and American plans.

Metropole Hotel; Kiangse and Foochow Roads; European and American plans.

The Shanghai Municipal Orchestra

Palace Hotel; The Bund and Nanking Road; single, $12; double, $24; suites by arrangement.

Park Hotel; Bubbling Well and Park Roads; American plan; single, $12; double, $22.

Hotel-apartments:—

Blackstone Apartments; 1331 Rte. Lafayette; single, $10; double, $18.

Bubbling Well Home; Lane 591, 196 Bubbling Well Road; daily, weekly and monthly rates by application.

China United Apartments; 104 Bubbling Well Road; single, $12, double, $16.

Cathay Mansions; Rue Cardinal Mercier and Rue Bourgeat (French Concession); single, $10; double, $18.

"Medhurst," 934 Bubbling Well Road, terms per day, including all meals and full service, single $10 to $12; double $16 to $18. Special rates for permanent residents.

CLUBS

There are so many clubs and associations, of so many different nationalities, in Shanghai that there is no reason why the visitor should not be able to make friendly contacts. Properly introduced, strangers may readily obtain temporary privileges of membership.

The Shanghai Club.—The fame of the Shanghai Club and its reputed "longest bar in the world" is international. It is located at 3 The Bund. A British institution, other nationals are admitted to membership. On being proposed and seconded by members, visitors may have the privileges of the club for fourteen days, but not more than three times in a year. Members of the Bengal, Singapore, and Hongkong clubs have visitors' privileges.

Country Club.—The Country Club, 651 Bubbling Well Road, is purely social. The Club has been laid out with extensive lawns, flower beds, and ornamental water. It has a swimming pool and tennis courts. Strangers in Shanghai, proposed and seconded by two or more members, are admitted for a period not exceeding ten days.

American Club. — The American Club, 209 Foochow Road, is a centre of American life in Shanghai, but, like the Shanghai Club, accepts other nationals for membership. A unique feature is that women are not admitted except on the annual Ladies' Night and when, occasionally, the annual "Washington's Birthday Ball" is held at the club. The club is well equipped, with living quarters for a limited number of members. Transients, properly nominated and seconded, are accorded all privileges, except voting, for a period of two weeks.

Columbia Country Club. — The Columbia Country Club, 301 Great Western Road, is an American club, purely social, although, as in the case of most Shanghai clubs, membership is not limited by racial lines. This "country" club is really in the country. It is

particularly attractive in the Summer with its spacious verandah and swimming pool. All the usual club facilities are available. There are limited living accommodations for male members. The customary privileges are extended to properly introduced visitors.

Cercle Sportif Francais. — The Cercle Sportif Francais ("French Club") at 290 Route Cardinal Mercier is the most cosmopolitan in membership of any club in Shanghai. Women members are limited to forty and there are always many on the waiting list. This club is both sporting and social. There is a roof garden for dancing in the Summer and in the Winter there are usually Sun-

The Shanghai Club

day afternoon tea dances in the ballroom on the first floor. There is also a swimming pool. Masculine visitors in Shanghai may obtain privileges by the customary procedure. Army and navy officers of all European countries and America are automatically members simply by "signing in the book." Ladies who are relatives of members of the French Club may also become temporary members.

Deutscher Garten Klub.—The German Garden Club at 454 Avenue Haig is the sports and social gathering place for the German community in Shanghai. Visitors are accorded privileges.

Masonic Club.—The Masonic Club, formed in 1882, has its headquarters at 93 Canton Road. Masons in Shanghai are glad to propose visiting brethren.

American University Club.—This club, as indicated by the name, is open for students, former or active, of American universities. It meets from time to time (always announced in the local press) for banquets, rallies, or dances. Applicants should communicate with Mr. J. B. Lee. Secretary, P. O. Box 1982.

Rotary Club.—Rotary Club headquarters in Shanghai are at 133 Yuen Ming Yuen Road. Weekly tiffins are held at the Metropole Hotel on Thursdays with speeches from visiting or resident Rotarians.

Women's Clubs.—Women's clubs in Shanghai are legion and take in almost every nationality. The outstanding women's clubs are the American Women's Club, 577 Bubbling Well Road; British

Women's Association, Hongkong and Shanghai Bank building on The Bund; the German Women's Benevolent Society which meets at the Deutscher Garten Klub, 454 Avenue Haig; the Netherlands Ladies' Club at 1271 Rue Lafayette, and the Portuguese Women's Association at the Pearce Apartments, Boone and Chapoo Roads. When visitors in Shanghai are brought to their attention by members they are always eager to invite them to their gatherings.

Y.M. & W.C.A.'S

Foreign Y.M.C.A. headquarters are located at 150 Bubbling Well Road; the Navy Y.M.C.A. is at 630 Szechuen Road; the International branch of the Y.W.C.A., 55 Yuen Ming Yuen Road; the Japanese Y.M.C.A., 206 Range Road; Chinese Y.M.C.A. headquarters, 599 Szechuen Road and 123 Boulevard de Montigny, and the Chinese Y.W.C.A., 55 Yuen Ming Yuen Road.

American Club

Veranda of Cercle Sportif Francais

GOLF

Hongkew Golf Club	Hongkew Park
Hungjao Golf Club	Hungjao & Rubicon Roads
Hungjao Ladies' Golf Club	Hungjao & Rubicon Roads
Kiangwan Country Club (Golf)	295 Boone Road (c/o Japanese Club)
Shanghai Golf Club	Seekingjao, Kiangwan

RIDING

Ponies may be rented by the day or by the hour at the riding schools in Shanghai. Pony riding is a favourite Sunday morning pastime in Shanghai, the quiet outlying roads, Great Western Road, Warren Road, Columbia Road, Hungjao Road, Jessfield Road, Brenan Road, and the Rubicon being much in demand for this purpose. Ponies may be had at the following places:

Ascot Riding School, 700 Tunsin Road.

Columbia and Great Western Riding Academy, 470 Great Western Road.

Haig Riding School, 765 Avenue Haig.

Paper-hunting. — Paper-hunting is a popular sport among cross-country riders, and well attended meets under the auspices of the Shanghai Paper Hunt Club are held at week-ends during the season.

MILADY GOES A-SHOPPING

For women who like to go shopping — they all do — Shanghai is a Paradise. It has all the attractions of Paris, and more. A most marvellous range of merchandise and curios awaits inspection. Silks and satins and silver, jewels and jades, furs and furbelows, linens and lingerie, trunks and trinkets, shoes and sealing wax, embroideries and embellishments — the shops are full of treasure trove dear to the feminine heart and prices, gauged by European

and American standards, are very reasonable.

It is impossible to outline a definite, fixed shopping district. On Avenue Joffre, Yates Road, Nanking Road, Bubbling Well Road and elsewhere, speciality shops flourish, Many reliable shops have advertised their wares in "All About Shanghai and Environs"; they may safely be recommended as to quality and prices.

Information on Jade.—Chinese jewellery is a fascinating item, with its vari-coloured precious and semi-precious stones and fantastic designs. Then there is jade. There are two varieties of this stone. Nephrite is a dull green and Jadeite is a lovely, clear applegreen. Jade is to be had in various other colours; white, blue, pink, yellow and brown, but the nearer it approaches the colour of the emerald the more authentic and valuable it is. Usually this very hard stone is intricately carved and fashioned into pendants, rings, brooches or earrings. Jade may be found all over Shanghai but it is advised to patronize the better known and advertised shops. Do not buy jade in the Chinese City unless you are an expert.

The craft of the Chinese silversmith is unique, and produces the most intricate and elaborate examples of Chinese patience and skill. Silverware may be purchased at surprisingly low prices, tea and coffee sets, cigarette cases, rickshaws, junks, sampans, and pagodas are wrought in silver.

Silks and Furs.—The silks and brocades are gorgeous in every weave, design and colour. The brocades are particularly suitable for evening wraps and negligees. There are soft crepes in dainty pastel tones for the more intimate garments and rich,

heavy silks and satins in deep, warm tones of plum and peach and old burgundy. Chinese silk is exceptionally cheap and may be had in every colour. Men will be interested in the heavy Chinese pongee.

Furs may be had very reasonably. Many of them are imported from Siberia, Manchuria and Mongolia. The favourite (and in other countries almost priceless) silver fox is here within the reach of all visitors. There are sables, otter and stone marten; among the cheaper pelts the white and red fox, beaver, grey and platinum squirrel, marmot, and many others. They may all be purchased by the pelt or already made up.

One of the largest and most profitable industries of China is lace-making. Lace is cheap and much of it is beautiful. Lace from France and Belgium may also be bought in Shanghai at comparatively low prices. Mandarin robes are very popular among the ladies for evening cloaks. There are countless lace and embroidery shops in Shanghai. (*See* the classified business directory in this book).

For the home there are wall hangings of exquisite embroidery, beautiful old prints, and furniture, either old or new. Many visitors to Shanghai will take home enough furniture for a Chinese room.

Lingerie is to be had in every style and shade and will be made to your own design and fancy in a few hours.

*   *   *

Modern Women. — The old tradition of China, that women were made to remain behind the scenes, unheard, and practically unseen save by the man who "owned" them, is rapidly becoming a thing of the past. To-day many Chinese women are actively engaged in business. For instance there is the Women's Commercial & Savings Bank, 392 Nanking Road, which is entirely owned, managed, and run by Chinese women. Thousands of Chinese girls to-day earn their own living as stenographers or shop girls. And the thousands of cabaret dancing girls, who are continually in the public eye, are conclusive evidence that another old tradition of China has been completely shattered.

Chapter Nine
COMMUNICATIONS

RADIO AND CABLE

RADIO and cable communication facilities in Shanghai are reliable. All traffic offices for either radio or cable are under the control of the Bureau of International Telegraphs. Radio offices are centrally located in Sassoon House (Cathay Hotel) with a branch office at 15 Avenue Edward VII.

The traffic offices for cablegrams are at 34 Avenue Edward VII, opposite the radio branch office. The branch office for cablegrams is at 27 Peking Road.

In Sassoon House are the Chinese Government Radio Administration and the Shanghai Coast Station, with their traffic offices. In the same building are the R.C.A. Communications, Inc., subsidiary of Radio Corporation of America, and the Mackay Radio and Telegraph Co. Both of them are the transmitting companies of the Chinese Government Radio Administration. The traffic offices at 34 Avenue Edward VII for cables are three in number, Great Northern Telegraph Co., Ltd.; Eastern Extension, Australasia and China Telegraph Co., Ltd., and Commercial Pacific Cable Co.

Cablegrams and radiograms from Shanghai without any special service indication are rated per word in Shanghai dollar cents (effective from June 1, 1934) as follows:

Manila	1.00	New York	4.50
Honolulu	3.50	Europe (except Russia)	3.45
Sydney	3.35	Moscow	2.00
Wellington	3.75	Vladivostock	1.50
Vancouver	4.30	Buenos Aires	6.70
Ottawa	4.60	Tokyo	0.75
San Francisco	3.75	Hongkong	0.28
Chicago	4.35	All North China	0.20

Messages in code (five letters per word or less) are charged at six-tenths ordinary rate with a minimum charge of five words for each telegram. Thus the word rate to London being $3.45, the code-word rate is $2.07.

Urgent messages, having priority, must be clearly marked and are charged at double the ordinary rate. Deferred messages are charged at half the ordinary rate. Lettergrams (minimum 25 words) are charged at one-third the ordinary rate. Deferred messages are not accepted for China, Hongkong or Japan.

Telegraph traffic offices are co-operating with post offices, at Shanghai. Radiograms or cablegrams may be filed at almost every post office.

Differences in Time should be taken into consider-ation in calculating time of delivery. When it is noon in Shanghai (according to the official time chart of the Chinese Government Radio Administration) in the following places it is: —

New York	11.00 p.m. previous day.
Chicago	10.00 p.m. previous day.
San Francisco	8.00 p.m. previous day.
Honolulu	5.30 p.m. previous day.
Japan	1.00 p.m. same day.
Australia	2.00 p.m. same day.
Russia	6.00 a.m. same day.
Berlin	5.00 a.m. same day.
London	4.00 a.m. same day.

POSTAL SERVICES

Only a little over a decade ago there were seven separate Post Offices in Shanghai, as most of the countries then represented here maintained their own mail services. Today the Head Post Office at the corner of Soochow and North Szechuen Roads, under the control of the Directorate General of Posts, which also controls the postal services over the whole country, handles all Chinese and foreign mail matter entering and leaving Shanghai, the foreign mail being that of the forty-eight nationalities represented here.

The Post Office maintains registered express delivery and insured mail (for letters and parcels) services. Express articles for China may be posted either as registered or ordinary mail matter but for abroad must be registered.

The following are the rates charged for the main services:

1. — ORDINARY:

		Letters	*Post Cards*
	Local	2 cts.	1 ct.
	China	5 "	2 ½ cts.
	Hongkong and Japan	5 "	2 ½ "
	Foreign	25 "	5 "

2. — REGISTERED *(additional to ordinary)*:

	China	6 cts.
	Europe	25 "
	United States	25 "
	Japan	6 "

3. — EXPRESS *(additional to ordinary)*:

	China	12 cts.
	Hongkong	No service
	Japan (must also be registered)	12 cts.
	Foreign (must also be registered)	50 "

4. — INSURED *(additional to ordinary & registration)*:

	China	1 %
	Japan	10 cts. for each $120
	Foreign	50 " " " 300 Gold Frs.

5. — AIR-MAIL *(additional)*:

	Nanking	25 cts.
	Hankow	25 "
	Tientsin	25 "
	Peiping	25 "
	Canton	50 "

Postal Remittances and Savings Bank. — A remarkable and highly successful development of the Chinese Postal Service is the Postal Remittances and Savings Bank, a government institution of great efficiency, which is rendering invaluable service to millions of people. Particulars of international remittances, as issued in the Bank's Annual Report, will be of special interest to the visitor to Shanghai.

The total number and value of international money orders issued in 1933 were 25,319 and $1,431,660.58, respectively, while the total number and value of international money orders cashed were 40,772 and $1,979,886.11, respectively. The Postal Remittances and Savings Bank is one of the few institutions in the world which will honour a draft for less than $50. It is conducting a regular and efficient banking business, paying interest at 4 ½ per cent. on current savings accounts and six to seven per cent. on fixed savings accounts for one to two years.

Air Mail Service.—Another successful development of the postal service is that of air mail lines, tariffs for which have been quoted in the foregoing tables. The China National Aviation Corporation transports air mail to Nanking, Hankow, Tientsin, Peiping, and Canton. The last named service is of particular value inasmuch as it makes possible the delivery of letters to Europe almost a week sooner than by steamer. The distance to Canton, 960 air miles, is covered by plane in ten hours. From Canton mail is taken to Singapore by steamer where it is again taken by air and delivered in Europe in eleven days. (Canton service temporarily suspended).

AIRWAYS

Ancient China, in recent years, has become air-minded, and foreign planes are being imported in large numbers for military, commercial, and air mail services.

It is now possible to travel to almost any large city in China within a few hours, safely and comfortably. Airways are controlled by the Chinese National Government. Private flying is not allowed. The China National Aviation Corporation, in which the Pacific American Airways Co. is interested, has a service running North and South from Shanghai and into the interior of China. The extension of the southern service to Manila is contemplated.

The Eurasia Aviation Corporation is a transport company controlled by the Chinese Government and has weekly service to Lanchow, a city in the interior of China just South of Mongolia. Due to political disturbances the line which formerly ran to Tchukuchak was discontinued at this point. It is, therefore, difficult to make train connections to Europe. It is hoped to re-establish the former line to Tchukuchak (where European connections are made) in the near future. Bi-monthly mail and passenger service to Peiping is maintained by this company.

The China National Aviation Corporation has aerodromes at Shanghai, Nanking, Anking, Kiukiang, Hankow, Shasi, Ichang, Wanhsien, Chungking, Chengtu, Haichow, Tsingtao, Tientsin, Peiping, Wenchow, Foochow, Amoy, Swatow, and Canton.

Over the Gorges by Air. — A recommended air flight is up the Yangtsze River over the stupendous Yangtsze Gorges. This trip may also be made by river steamer but requires three weeks, whereas the air trip takes but four days, with overnight stops at Hankow. This round trip costs $780 in local currency. Cities passed on this trip are Nanking, the capital of China; Anking, seat of the Government of Anhwei Province; Kiukiang, Hankow, "The Collecting Place of Nine Provinces;" Shasi, Ichang, a walled city in the midst of a wild, mountainous region; Wanhsien, noted for junk trade and, finally, Chungking, the end of the line, a city surrounded by a wall a hundred feet high.

In flying from Shanghai to Peiping the cities of Tsingtao and Tientsin are passed while the Shanghai-Canton line takes in Wen-

chow, Foochow, Amoy, and Swatow.

Names of Streets. — In the International Settlement of Shanghai the streets running parallel to The Bund are named after the provinces of China while those intersecting them are named after cities.

*   *   *

The population of China is estimated at about one-third of the world total.

*   *   *

Kiangsu Province, of which Shanghai is the capital, has an area of 45,000 square miles, Shanghai approximately 30 square miles.

*   *   *

"Cumsha" (tips) to servants is expected from foreigners for practically every service. It is a custom but it may easily be overdone. You don't tip a servant for lighting a cigarette but you do tip him for fetching a drink.

*   *   *

Chinese, on the whole, are bargainers but once their word is given they usually can be depended upon. If a Chinese says "can do" you may safely leave your order with him. When he says "no can" his word is final.

*   *   *

The average Chinese is a peaceable fellow, an agriculturist at heart, a pacifist almost always. A smile is almost always a passport to his friendship.

Chapter Ten
FINANCIAL INFORMATION

CHINESE CURRENCY

"**B**IG" and "Small" Money. — Fantastic as it may seem to the bewildered stranger in Shanghai, the currency of China is not really so complicated as it seems to be. Volumes have been written on the subject, but the visitor who is not likely to go far into the interior need not concern himself with all the complications which arise away from the main treaty ports.

Chinese currency is founded on the decimal system and is based on the national silver dollar (commonly known as "Mex."), convertible into paper notes of 10, 20 and 50 cents, known as "big money" in Shanghai, or into 10 and 20 cent silver coins, which are known as "small money" and whose relative value to the silver dollar varies from day to day. The customary rate is six 20-cent coins and a few coppers for a dollar.

There are troubles here also!

Bank notes are issued by various Chinese banks ranging in value from 1, 5, 10, 50 to 100 dollars. The number of coppers to a dollar varies from day to day, usually standing around 300, but these coins are only used by the poorer class and in travelling by bus and tram (though not essential, as paper notes are accepted), so the visitor need not worry about the vagaries of copper exchange.

Until 1933, major commercial transactions were usually carried out in terms of Taels, a unit of value based upon a shoe-shaped slug of silver, and whose relation to the dollar varied from day to day, but on April 5, 1933, the Government issued a decree prohibiting the use of this form of calculation, and the use of the Tael in reckoning commercial and official transactions, professional fees, rents, etc., is gradually being abandoned.

Coppers, Cash and Paper. — As a point of interest, although it will not financially concern the foreigner in Shanghai, Chinese coppers are once more divided into "cash," of which there are some 3,000 to a dollar. Cash may be small, circular coins with a square hole centered or they may be silver paper in pyramid shape which are usually carried on bamboo poles swung across a shoulder. "Cash" is the only form of money which circulates throughout all of China, other monies differing in various provinces and varying in exchange value. Paper "cash" are popular among the Chinese as "joss" (prayer) offerings to the gods and departed souls.

The newcomer in Shanghai will occasionally find himself in the possession of spurious silver coins. The initiated can usually tell by the ring of a coin whether it is good or bad.

Unification of Currency. — The first step toward unifying the currency of China was taken on March 1, 1933, with the opening of the National Government Central Mint, at the north end of Gordon Road in Chapei. Up to the present time only the new standard dollar has been minted. It is planned later to make ten- and twenty-cent coins which will have the value of the present "big money" paper. In the near future there will be but five twenty-cent and ten ten-cent coins to the dollar.

At the present time all of the old silver dollars are being collected for the Mint by the banks for conversion into new dollars. The Mint now (July, 1934) makes 8,000,000 dollars a month and, in addition, casts silver bars which are distributed to banks for reserve. The bars are each worth $1,000 and two hundred bars are cast daily. There has been so much civil strife in China and so many political divisions that the coins of one province seldom are accepted in another. With the establishment of the National Government Central Mint it is hoped that the currency of China will eventually become standardized.

BANKS AND EXCHANGE

The vagaries of foreign exchange, further complicated by the "big" and "small" money of Chinese currency, are bewildering to the stranger in Shanghai. There is perhaps a wider range of foreign exchange in Shanghai than in any other place in the world. Any known sound currency can readily be converted into Chinese money, or vice versa. But be sure you are obtaining the proper rate.

There are hundreds of small native banks and exchange shops scattered throughout the city and as the minor Chinese financier calculates his profits on an excessively thin margin many old residents find it advantageous to give them their exchange business. But the stranger — and how promptly the Chinese can identify him — is advised to take his financial problems to the larger and more responsible banks. This also gives additional protection against counterfeit money, which is abundant in Shanghai.

Reputable Banks. — There are in Shanghai a large number of foreign and Chinese banks where the stranger will be received with the same courtesy and service as in London, Paris, or New York. In the appended lists will be found the names and addresses of the principal banks. What are known as the Chinese "modern-style" banks are concerns which conduct all the usual activities of foreign banks, in distinction from the "native banks," institutions which also hold a very important place in the field of finance, but whose activities are confined to purely commercial transactions. The Chinese banks listed in this chapter are "modern-style" banks, but in addition to the ordinary routine of banking practice, as followed in foreign countries, they also maintain "native bank" departments and it is upon this section of the Chinese banking community that much of the smooth working of Shanghai's vast commercial machinery depends.

Among the more important foreign financial institutions are: —

American Express Co.	158 Kiukiang Rd.
American Oriental Banking Corp.	29 Nanking Rd.
Banque Belge Pour L'Etranger	20 The Bund.
Banque de l'Indochine	29 The Bund.
Banque Franco-Chinese	1 French Bund,
Chartered Bank of India, Australia and China	18 The Bund.
Chase Bank	80 Kiukiang Rd.
Cook and Son, Ltd., Thos.	Szechuen & Nanking Roads
Deutsch-Asiatische Bank	294 Szechuen Rd.
Hongkong & Shanghai Banking Corp.	12 The Bund
Italian Bank for China	186 Kiukiang Road
Mercantile Bank of India, Ltd.	26 The Bund
Mitsubishi Bank, Ltd.	36 Kiukiang Rd.
Mitsui Bank, Ltd.	60 Kiukiang Rd.
National City Bank of New York	41 Kiukiang Rd.
Nederlandsch Indische Handels-Bank	255 Kiangse Rd.
Netherlands Trading Society	Sassoon House
P. & O. Banking Corp.	6 The Bund
Sumitomo Bank, Ltd.	69 Kiukiang Rd.

Among the more important "modern style" Chinese banks are: —

Bank of Canton, Ltd.	52 Ningpo Rd.
Bank of China	22 The Bund
Bank of Communications	14 The Bund
Bank of East Asia, Ltd.	299 Szechuen Rd.
Chekiang Industrial Bank, Ltd.	159 Hankow Rd.

China Banking Corp.	Szechuen & Foochow Rds.
China State Bank, Ltd.	342 Peking Rd.
China & South Sea Bank, Ltd.	110 Hankow Rd.
Chung Foo Union Bank	103 Jinkee Rd.
Commercial Bank of China	7 The Bund
Continental Bank	113 Kiukiang Rd.
Joint Savings Society	261 Szechuen Rd.
Kincheng Banking Corp.	200 Kiangse Rd.
Manufacturers' Bank of China, Ltd.	50 Hankow Rd.
National Commercial Bank, Ltd.	280 Peking Rd.
Oversea-Chinese Banking Corp., Ltd.	120 Kiukiang Rd.
Shanghai Commercial & Savings Bank, Ltd.	50 Ningpo Rd.

Banking Resources. — Latest available banking statistics show that the combined paid-up capital of 29 leading Chinese banks in Shanghai is $156,777,676 (Mex.). These 29 banks are considered to be the largest and most important. Statistics of these banks are as follows:

	(Mex.)
Combined Capital	$156,777,676
Reserve Fund and Surplus	51,876,210
Current Accounts and Fixed Deposits	1,974,097,476
Drafts Issued	21,290,781
Notes in Circulation	430,482,554

With the exception of the American-Oriental Banking Corporation, which is owned and controlled in Shanghai, all foreign banks are branches affiliated with parent banks in other lands. Major items in the American-Oriental statement are:

Capital (Paid-up)	$2,832,733	(Mex.)
Surplus and Undivided Profits	2,472,938	"
Deposits	9,330,435	"

Exchange Rates.—Exchange rates fluctuate daily, with some amazing ups and downs. At one time, not long after the World War, the American dollar purchased only ninety cents Mex.; early in 1933 an American dollar was worth $5.15 (Mex.) At this writing (July, 1934) the American dollar approximates $2.90 (Mex.) There is a vast amount of speculation in exchange, gold, and silver in Shanghai. It is, in large part, a mechanism for gambling on a gigantic scale. Fortunes are won and lost in exchange.

In the subjoined table the amounts quoted concern the Pound Sterling and the American dollar. Each quotation is the equivalent of one Shanghai dollar:

	Sterling	*Gold*
March, 1929	1 | 10	.429
March, 1930	1 | 4½	.339
March, 1931	- | 11½	.227
March, 1932	1 | 3½	.236
March, 1933	1 | 2½	.208
March, 1934	1 | 4½	.35

Brokers and Markets.—For those who wish to "play the market" Shanghai offers a wide variety of entertainment. There is local and foreign speculation in commodities and stocks, gold bars and silver. Prompt execution of orders is given in all the leading and most of the minor markets of the world. London, Paris and New York stocks are quoted, as well as local issues, of which there are many, both bonds and shares.

Owing to the difference in time, closing quotations on the New York Stock Exchange are available in Shanghai very early in the morning.

No matter where your home may be, in Shanghai you can establish close and accurate connection with the markets in which you are interested.

Among the leading Shanghai brokerage houses are: —

American Oriental Finance Corp.	29 Nanking Rd.
Benjamin & Potts	27 The Bund
Bisset & Co., J.P.	12 The Bund
Levy & Co., S.E.	113 Kiukiang Rd.
Rosenfeld & Son, A.B.	113 Kiukiang Rd.
Shahmoon & Co., E.E.	113 Kiukiang Rd.
Swan, Culbertson & Fritz	Sassoon House
Toeg, S.E.	113 Kiukiang Rd.
White & Co.	60 Kiukiang Rd.
Yuan Yeh & Co.	255 Peking Rd.

REAL ESTATE AND BUILDING

Shanghai, one of the fastest growing of the world's larger cities — the modern city is largely a development of the last twenty years — has a lively and active real estate market, with a huge volume of building. The Sino-Japanese fighting of early 1932 gave a severe setback to development, but the onward rush has been resumed. Real estate transactions were placed at $90,000,000 in 1930, $183,000,000 in 1931, $25,200,000 in 1932 (the "war" year) and $43,000,000 in 1933.

Shanghai, in which is concentrated the wealth of North China, has ample funds for development projects of merit. As a matter of fact, the banks are "over-loaded" with money (silver).

Building construction is at a high level in Shanghai. A tremendous amount of work is always under way, come bad times or good.

Building Values. — In the International Settlement alone, building permits issued in 1933 were for 5,130 structures as against 3,439 in 1932. These buildings represented an estimated value of $35,000,000. The peak year in building was 1930 when an estimate was made by the Shanghai Municipal Council of $65,000,000.

Total Values for Shanghai. — The value of new buildings in the entire Shanghai area, including the Municipality of Greater Shanghai (Chinese), International Settlement, and French Concession, has been as follows: 1929, $63,000,000; 1930, $100,000,000; 1931, $87,000,000; 1932. $50,000,000; 1933, $72,000,000.

New buildings for which permits were issued in the International Settlement during the year 1933, compared with four preceding years, were classified as follows:

Description:	1933	1932	1931	1930	1929
Chinese houses	3,545	2,071	6,987	6,818	5,282
Foreign residences	257	95	97	327	380
Hotels	—	3	2	3	1
Apartment buildings	13	5	9	5	8
Office buildings	13	21	41	35	33
Foreign stores	204	216	273	298	310

Aerial View of Race Course and Public Recreation Ground and Surroundings (Photo by C. de Soria, courtesy of N.C.D.N.)

Theatres	4	2	4	6	6
Schools	7	—	5	6	1
Cotton mills	—	6	4	3	3
Factories	27	28	73	24	50
Other Industrial Buildings	63	23	28	38	24
Godowns	20	27	27	64	52
Garages	98	48	158	75	116
Miscellaneous	879	894	991	1,134	1,321
Totals	5,130	3,439	8,699	8,836	7,586

Value: 1933, \$35,543,740; 1932, \$25,454,600; 1931, \$52,258,101; 1930, \$65,287,320; 1929, \$35,209,566.

Real Estate Brokers.—Shanghai real estate offers many attractions to the prudent investor.

It is interesting to note that shortly after the promulgation of the first Land Regulations in 1845, land on The Bund sold at from \$50 to \$60 a mow (7,260 square feet under original definition).

Among the more important real estate agents and firms are:

Asia Realty Co. (Fed. Inc., U.S.A.)	50 Nanking Road
Brandt & Rodgers, Ltd.	391 Kiangse Road
Cathay Land Co.. Ltd.	Sassoon House
China Realty Co. (Fed. Inc., U.S.A.)	290 Szechuen Road
Credit Foncier d'Extreme Orient	18 The Bund
Cumine & Co., Ltd.	149 Szechuen Road China
Fonciere et Immobiliere de Chine	9 Ave. Edward VII
Metropolitan Land Co., Ltd.	81 Jinkee Road
Nissim, N. Fred	278 Kiangse Road
Realty Investment Co. (Fed. Inc., U.S.A.)	210 Szechuen Road
Shanghai Land Investment Co., Ltd.,	100 Jinkee Road

The first iron bridge over the Soochow Creek, forerunner of the present Garden Bridge, was built in 1871. It collapsed during the final stages of construction.

* * *

Shanghai's first foreign gaol was built in 1856, in the compound of the British Consulate. By courtesy of the British authorities, it provided lodgement for American prisoners as well as British! It has been suggested that this was the beginning of Anglo-American understanding in the management of the Settlement.

* * *

The first Shanghai Club, which occupied the same site as the present building, was erected in 1862.

Chapter Eleven
GENERAL INFORMATION

CLIMATE

HONESTY compels the statement that climate is not one of the attractions of Shanghai. It is very hot and humid in the Summer and quite cold in the Winter. Twice a year, in the Spring and in the Fall, there are periods of several weeks when weather conditions are very pleasant. January is the coldest month, July the hottest. In general, Shanghai's climate has been described as "one-third of the year tropical and two-thirds temperate."

"It isn't the heat, it's the humidity," is a trite quotation but it is frequently aptly used in Shanghai, the average annual humidity being 82.2. During late August and early September, the "typhoon season," there is likely to be much rain if not many typhoons, which usually pass by giving Shanghai scant attention.

Temperature Fahrenheit	Degrees
Average annual temperature (over 60 years)	59.34
Average monthly highest (July)	97.29
Average monthly lowest (January)	43.27
Average annual highest temperature	98.96
Average annual lowest temperature	45.05

Humidity	
Average annual relative humidity	82.2
Average monthly highest	84.2
Average monthly lowest	76.3

Rainfall Averages			
January	49.9 mm	July	148.2 mm
February	57.9 mm	August	145.7 mm
March	86.2 mm	September	123.9 mm
April	91.6 mm	October	74.5 mm
May	90.5 mm	November	50.4 mm
June	184.8 mm	December	35.6 mm

Fahrenheit Temperature.—In Fahrenheit, the average temperature for the first quarter is 40.2; second quarter, 63.8; third quarter, 76.2; fourth quarter, 52.5. During July and early August the mid-day temperature usually hovers between 90 and 100 degrees, with a high average of humidity. Most of the rainfall is during the Summer. There is very little snow, but considerable sleet in the Winter.

Shanghai's coldest year was recorded in 1893 when a low of 10 degrees Fahrenheit was registered in January. On January 10, 1930, the next coldest day was recorded with 12 degrees. Such Winters in China are termed "four coat Winters" by the Chinese.

The present year (1934) has broken high temperature records for Shanghai. On July 1 the thermometer rose to 102.7 degrees Fahr., the highest for sixty years, and on July 12 it reached 104.4, the highest ever registered in the city.

Taken by months the best season is from the middle of September to December. January is always cold. February and March are variable. April is Spring-like. May and June are usually delightful. July, August, and the first half of September are hot and moist, and rains and typhoons are welcomed to break the heat.

Chinese Forecasts.—The Chinese predict the weather according to their calendar "moons," which are difficult to compare with the Occidental calendar as they vary from year to year. Generally speaking, the Chinese changes in weather are designated as follows:

Slight cold (Hsiao-han)	Early January
Great cold (Ta-han)	Late January
Beginning of Spring (Li-chun)	Early February
Rain Water (Yu-shui)	Middle February
Excited Insects (Ching-che)	Early March
Vernal Equinox (Chun-fen)	Late March
Pure Brightness (Ching-ming)	Early April
Corn Rain (Ku-yu)	Late April
Beginning of Summer (Li-hsia)	Early May
Small Fullness (Hsiao-man)	Late May
Sprouting Seeds (Mang-chung)	Early June
Summer Solstice (Hsia-chih)	Late June
Slight Heat (Hsiao-shu)	Early July
Great Heat (Ta-shu)	Late July
Beginning Autumn (Li-chiu)	Early August
Stopping of Heat (Chu-shu)	Late August
White Dew (Pai-lu)	Early September
Autumnal Equinox (Chiu-fen)	Late September
Cold Dew (Han-lu)	Early October
Frost Descent (Shuang-chiang)	Late October
Beginning of Winter (Li-tung)	Early November
Slight Snow (Hsiao-hsueh)	Late November
Great Snow (Ta-hsueh)	Early December
Winter Solstice (Tung-chih)	Late December

What to Wear. — Visitors to Shanghai during June, July, August and early September will want a completely tropical wardrobe. White suits are suitable for men and the sheerest of summer frocks for women. Sandals are usually worn by Shanghai women while stockings may be dispensed with altogether. The general rule for Summer underclothes is the fewer the better.

During December, January and February heavy clothing is required. The intermediate months of March, April and May; September, October and November, require medium weight clothing, such as is usually worn in America and Europe at the same time of year.

Tropical Latitude. — Although in mid-Winter it is difficult to believe, Shanghai has approximately the same Latitude as Cairo, Egypt, and Morocco, is a little South of the Bermudas, and falls roughly on the same parallel as Charleston, South Carolina, and Los Angeles, California.

HOW TO KEEP WELL

While the ordinary rules for the maintenance of health apply in Shanghai as elsewhere, certain precautions in the matter of food and hygiene should be taken by both visitors and residents. Among the precautions recommended by the Public Health Department of the Municipal Council are:

Vaccination every three years; inoculation against typhoid every two years, and inoculation against cholera every Summer.

Don't consume foodstuffs which are not fresh and which have not recently been cooked, boiled or otherwise sterilized.

Fresh meat is stamped with the official stamp of the Council. Beef, mutton and pork are marked in two grades, first quality in purple, second quality in blue.

If vegetables of local origin, such as lettuce, tomatoes, onions, radishes, etc., are eaten raw, they should be thoroughly washed and then sterilized by dipping in boiling water.

Fruit is a constant source of danger during the Summer months, but it is a problem that has to be faced. Such fruits as apples, oranges, grapefruit, bananas, watermelon and pears which possess undamaged thick skins are safe, provided care is taken to cleanse the external surface before eating. Other and thinner skinned fruits, such as grapes, strawberries, raspberries and the like, and apricots and peaches are safe only if eaten cooked. The popular method of dipping fruit in a solution of potassium permanganate is not recommended since it is far less reliable than boiling water.

Shell fish should never be eaten raw, and are best avoided altogether.

No milk other than pasteurized milk or grade "A., T. T. Raw," should be consumed without boiling.

For absolute safety, drinking water should be boiled.

Be moderate in the consumption of alcoholic drinks and follow the "Sundown" rule in the Summer months. Get your supplies from reliable sources.

Iced drinks should be consumed slowly.

Shanghai Summers can be made quite tolerable by observation of the following rules:

1. Use discretion in keeping out of the sun.
2. Wear light, loose and open clothing, light hats and shoes, and underwear of open texture. Wear loose collars, and do not keep your belt too tight.
3. Keep the air circulating in your room but do not sit directly in front of or under the fan. Expose yourself by all means to the night air, but keep your stomach well covered. Guard against chill.
4. Take moderate exercise. Over-exertion may produce just the condition you are trying to avoid.
5. When it is possible, take a short nap in the afternoon.
6. Do not over-eat, especially at mid-day. You need less food in the summer than you do in the winter.

HOSPITALS

China Inland Mission Hospital	1531 Sinza Road
Concord Woman's Hospital	36 Rue Moliere
Country Hospital	17 Great Western Road
Hospital Ste. Marie	197 Route Pere Robert
Municipal Isolation Hospital (foreigners)	41 Range Road
Paulun Hospital	415 Burkill Road
Shanghai General Hospital	190 North Soochow Rd.
Shanghai Nursing Home	185 Route Dufour
Shanghai Sanitarium and Hospital	150 Rubicon Road

The Shanghai General and Country hospitals are the largest.

VITAL STATISTICS

Birth Registration.—Birth registration in Shanghai is very incomplete, most of the Chinese neglecting it entirely, and the foreigners in Shanghai usually register at their respective Consulates. As far as the Chinese are concerned, the majority of practitioners and hospitals are willing to co-operate but the fact remains that the majority of childbirths do not take place in a hospital and no doctor attends.

In 1933 there were 829 births among the foreign residents which were registered — 423 males and 406 females. This represents a rate of 17.87 per 1,000, against 16.16 in 1932. In this year the birth rate was published for the first time, statistics having been assembled as a result of the co-operation of the medical profession and the hospitals.

Only 1,192 births among the Chinese were registered — 640 males and 552 females.

In 1933 deaths of foreigners in Shanghai totalled 661, of whom 524 were residents. The death rate was 11.29 per thousand, compared with 12.82 in 1932.

Deaths of children under one year were 15 per cent. of the total, the chief causes being pneumonia, diseases of early infancy and beri-beri.

Abandoned Bodies. — Some 5,715 Chinese deaths are included under the heading, "Exposed Corpses." They are the "unwanted" bodies of beggars, indigents, still-born children and female infants, etc., which are left on vacant lots for collection and burial by benevolent societies. It is impossible to give a detailed analysis of the causes of these deaths as there is no compulsory registration of deaths in Shanghai.

CHURCHES
Protestant

All Saints' Church
  (American Episcopal)   Rue Lafayette and Chapsal
Holy Trinity Cathedral
  (Church of England)   219 Kiukiang Road
Church of St. Andrew
  (Missions to Seamen)   171 Broadway
Church of Our Saviour   502 Dixwell Road
Community Church   53 Avenue Petain

Deutsche Evangelische Kirche	Avenue Haig and Great Western Road
Endeavourers' Church	Range and Chapoo Rds.
First Church of Christ, Scientist	178 Route Dufour, (American Masonic Temple)
Fourth Marines Church	Avenue Joffre and Rue Cardinal Mercier (Cathay Theatre)
Seventh Day Adventist Church, Central	526 Ningkuo Road
Shanghai Free Christian Church (Evangelical)	681 Hart Road
Union Church	107 Soochow Road

Roman Catholic

Church of Our Lady	694 Baikal Road
Church of the Sacred Heart	21 Nanzing Road
St. Joseph's Church	36 Rue Montauban

Russian Orthodox

Russian Orthodox Mission Church	55 Rue Paul Henry
St. Andrew's Church	220 Route Vallon
St. Nicholas Church	18 Rue Corneille

Jewish

Beth Aharon Synagogue	50 Museum Road
Ohel Moishe Synagogue	486 Seymour Road
Ohel Rachel Synagogue	200 Seymour Road

DAILY NEWSPAPERS

Foreign daily newspapers in Shanghai are in the English,

French, German and Russian languages. All, with the exception of the Shanghai Evening Post and Mercury, Ltd. (American daily) are morning papers.

Daily Newspapers:

North-China Daily News	17 The Bund
Shanghai Times	160 Ave. Edward VII
Evening Post and Mercury	17-21 Ave. Edward VII
China Press	11 Szechuen Road (Lane 126)
Le Journal de Shanghai (French)	21-23 Rue du Consulat
Deutsche Shanghai Zeitung (German)	Astor House (Room 96)
Shanghai Zaria (Russian)	774 Avenue Joffre
"Slovo" (Russian)	238 (1-2) Ave. du Roi Albert

PIDGIN ENGLISH

"Pidgin-English" is a curious jargon commonly used as a means of communication between the foreigner who has no knowledge of the Chinese language and the Chinese shopkeeper and servant with a limited knowledge of English.

Actually, the lingo is made up of a few English words (often mispronounced) expressed more or less in accordance with Chinese idiom. In spite of its limitations, it works surprisingly well. It is not as easy as it seems, however, and any Chinese can soon tell if you are a newcomer. Following are a few of the most frequently used phrases:

Maskee	Never mind
Talkee he	Tell him
No wantchee	I don't want that
Can do	That will do
No can do	That will not do
My no savvy	I don't understand
Pay my	Give it to me
Pay my look see	Let me look at it
Topside	Upstairs

Bottomside	Downstairs
Bym-bye makee pay	I'll pay later
Pay chow	Serve food
Catchee one piece rickshaw	Get a rickshaw
My wantchee	I want
My no wantchee	I don't want
Cumshaw	A tip
Catchee chop chop	Fetch quickly
No b'long plopper	This is not right
No squeeze	No overcharging
Walkee-walkee fish	Live fish
Joss House	Temple
Pay Master chit	Give Master the letter
B'long Shanghai side	To live in Shanghai
Chop chop	Quickly
B'long my pidgin	That's my business
Catchee baby	To have a baby
Learn piecee	Apprentice
Savvy box	Brain
How-fashion?	What for?
Amah	Chinese nurse or maid
Solly	Sorry
My catchee chow	I'm going to eat
Chit	A note or letter
What thing?	What is that?
This side	Here
Talkee my	Let me know
This b'long my	This is mine
What fashion no can?	Why not?
Talkee come morning time	Tell him to come in the morning
This b'long number one	This is very good
Three piece man come dinner	There will be three guests for dinner
S'pose no can do catchee coolie	If you can't do it get the coolie

Missy have got?	Is Mrs. — at home?
What side my room?	Where is my room?
This price b'long true?	Is this price genuine?
S'pose catchee two piece	Will it be cheaper to take
can more cheap?	two?
My wantchee walkee	I want to go for a walk
Pay two piece	Give me two
Can puttee book?	Is the bargain settled?

Pidgin English is not, as is optimistically believed by the visitor, made by adding "ee" to every word. "Pidgin" is a corruption of "business," so pidgin-English means business English. Many of the words, such as "Maskee," are of Portuguese derivation. "Junk" comes from the sound of "chueng" in the dialect of the coast where the Portuguese traded. Of Indian words we have "shroff," a dealer in money; "tiffin" for luncheon, "godown" for warehouse, "coolie" and "chit." There are a number of Chinese words included in pidgin-English such as "chow" for food, "chop" for stamp or receipt, and "cumshaw" for gratuity.

A good general rule to follow in speaking pidgin-English is to put the object first and use only the nominative case of pronouns, he and she. Use "my" for me, discard all grammar, and talk in roots of words and monosyllables. Do not try your pidgin English on every Chinese. If a Chinese can speak good English his dignity is highly offended if he is spoken to in pidgin. Try English first and if necessary break into your pidgin.

LOCAL TRANSPORTATION

Trams and Busses. — Shanghai utilities offer practically all modern transportation facilities except elevated and subway railways. Tramcars and motor-busses operate on regular schedules and routes throughout the International Settlement and French Concession and into Chinese territory, and by tram or bus, or both, it is possible to reach practically all points of interest in Shanghai. Rates are very reasonable, the service is fast and the vehicles are well maintained. For parties private buses carrying 22-25 persons may be hired from the transport firms at a charge of $5 per hour.

Hire Cars. — A number of excellent hire-car (taxicab) services are maintained. The usual minimum fare is $1 (Mex.) for about twenty minutes, and from $3 to $6 per hour, according to the type of car, etc. The chauffeur usually expects "cumsha" (a tip) of twenty cents for a trip up to half an hour.

Rickshaws and Rates. — The newcomer, especially if he has never been in the Orient before, probably will choose the omnipresent rickshaw for short trips about town. A rickshaw is almost always within range of one's voice and, to the stranger, the novelty of the man-drawn vehicle is an attraction.

It is well to know something about rickshaws and their "pullers" before engaging one. There are many foreigners in Shanghai who ruefully recall the time they paid a dollar gold for a ten-minute ride. Do not attempt to bargain with a rickshaw coolie with foreign money. Chinese money is all that means anything to him. And don't deliberately overpay him from a sense of sympathy. Rickshaw coolies live in dire poverty; pay them liberally but not foolishly, for it is an idiosyncrasy of the coolie mind to mistake generosity for idiocy.

If one wishes to engage a rickshaw by the day make arrangements through your hotel. The charge will be about $1.50, or $1 for half a day. For a ride of a few blocks pay ten cents; twenty cents for fifteen minutes; forty to sixty cents for an hour, according to distance travelled.

Don't go into strange territory in a rickshaw after dark; or make a careful note of the license number. Many rickshaw pullers solicit brazenly for places of bad repute at late hours.

Economic Transportation

Rickshaws bearing a S.M.C. (Shanghai Municipal Council) license can operate anywhere in the International Settlement or the French Concession. Those bearing a license in Chinese characters only are not permitted to enter the International Settlement.

Registration of public rickshaws is: International Settlement, 9,990; French Concession, 17,000; Nantao (Chinese City), 16,014; Chapei, 12,902; Western Area, 13,135.

Many Motor Cars.—The latest reports show 16,300 private motor cars licensed in Shanghai, 9,900 in the International Settlement and 6.400 in the French Concession. Only one license is required within the two foreign settlements, either International or French license serving in both districts. An additional license from the City Government of Greater Shanghai is required if the car is driven into Chinese territory.

WEIGHTS AND MEASURES

A few of the more familiar terms of weights and measures in vogue in Shanghai should be explained:

Li.—The Chinese unit of road measurement, equal to 1894.12 feet English. Like all Chinese measures it varies in different localities.

Catty.—A Malayan and Chinese weight unit equal to one and a third pounds avoirdupois.

Mow.—The Chinese unit of land measure. A Mow in Shanghai was defined by H.B.M. Consul in 1861 as the equivalent of 7,260 square feet English. As usual the measure varies greatly in different parts of the country and even in the same district two or more degrees of mow may be in use.

Picul.—The Chinese hundredweight, generally equal to 113 1/3 pounds avoirdupois.

CALENDAR

Officially China uses the same calendar system as Occidental countries, but only since 1912, when Dr. Sun Yat-sen became President of China. In reality, however, among the majority of Chinese the old lunar calendar system prevails. By the old method time is calculated by lunar months, consisting of 29 or 30 days each. Accordingly, twelve lunar months may total to either 354 or 355 days. The beginning of the year is determined by the sun, and New Year's Day must fall on the "first new moon after the sun enters Aquarius," which makes it come not before January 21, nor after February 19. When 12 lunar months do not meet the requirement for the beginning of another year an extra month is simply inserted. Each Chinese month begins with the new moon.

The Central Observatory at Peiping (Peking) which is a successor of the old Imperial Board of Astronomy, fixes the days on which hot or cold weather, rain, snow and frost may be expected and when different crops should be planted, by rules which appear to have been kept secret by the authorities of the Observatory. In all provinces Chinese farmers govern activities by these prophecies which, uncannily, are frequently correct.

CHINESE DYNASTIES

Dynasty	Began	Ended
Hsia	B.C. 2205	B.C. 1766
Shang	" 1766	" 1122
Chou	" 1122	" 249
Ch'in	" 249	" 206
Han	" 206	A.D. 25
Later Han	A.D. 25	" 221
The Three Kingdoms	" 221	" 265
Minor Han	" 221	" 265
Wei	" 220	" 265
Wu	" 229	" 265
Western Chin	" 265	" 317
Eastern Chin	" 317	" 420
Sung (House of Liu)	" 420	" 479
Ch'i	" 479	" 502
Liang	" 502	" 557
Ch'en	" 557	" 589

Sui	"	589	"	618
T'ang	"	618	"	907
The Five Dynasties	"	907	"	960
Posterior Liang	"	907	"	932
Posterior T'ang	"	932	"	936
Posterior Chin	"	936	"	947
Posterior Han	"	947	"	951
Posterior Chou	"	951	"	960
Liao	"	907	"	1125
Western Liao	"	1152	"	1168
Chin (Golden Tartars)	"	1115	"	1260
Sung	"	960	"	1127
Southern Sung	"	1127	"	1280
Yuan (Mongols)	"	1280	"	1368
Ming	"	1368	"	1644
Manchus	"	1644	"	1911
Shun Ch'ih	"	1644	"	1662
K'ang Hsi	"	1662	"	1723
Yung Cheng	"	1723	"	1736
Ch'en Lung	"	1736	"	1796
Chia Ch'ing	"	1796	"	1821
Tao Kuang	"	1821	"	1851
Hsien Feng	"	1851	"	1862
T'ung Chih	"	1862	"	1875
Kuang Hsu	"	1875	"	1908
Hsuan Tung	"	1908	"	1911

*   *   *

Watermelon Seeds. — Watermelon seeds are a favourite time-killing eatable among the Chinese. At formal parties and family entertainments watermelon seeds are always present. At banquets each guest has, among sauce dishes and wine cups, a plate of almonds and watermelon seeds. The idea is that the guest may divert himself between courses.

OFFICIAL INFORMATION

For authentic information of an official or semi-official nature, many sources are available in Shanghai, more particularly the Consulates, Chambers of Commerce, and foreign trade offices and bureaux.

Visitors, if they plan to remain more than a few days, are advised to register at their Consulates. It is both a protection and a convenience. Mail or cablegrams are frequently addressed to a traveller in care of his local Consulate, for instance. Passport advice may be had at your Consulate and this is of great importance. It is not always known, for instance, that only Japanese, Canadian, and Hongkong British visitors to Shanghai are exempt from Chinese visas on their passports. Travellers who are in Shanghai only for the period of their steamer stopover need not procure visas. Others must procure a visa each time Shanghai is entered. The Chinese Government charges the same fees for these visas as other governments charge to Chinese nationals. Thus the Chinese visa fee will differ widely, according to the nationality of the visitor. Consulates should be consulted in regard to all passport problems as one may blunder into needless difficulties through ignorance. Commercial and trade inquiries may likewise be made at the Consulates.

Consulates in Shanghai:

America (U.S.A.)	248-250 Kiangse Road
Austria	330 Szechuen Road
Belgium	1300 Rue Lafayette
Brazil	359 Route Cohen
Chile	Cathay Mansions
	(265 Rue Bourgeat)
Czechoslovakia	50 Route Amiral Courbet
Denmark	26 The Bund
Finland	100 Rue Marcel Tillot
France	2 Rue du Consulat
Germany	9-10 Whangpoo Road
Great Britain	33 The Bund
Italy	555 Bubbling Well Road
Japan	25A Whangpoo Road
Mexico	131 Museum Road
Netherlands	25 Rue du Consulat
Norway	110 Szechuen Road
Portugal	1050 Rue Lafayette
Russia	1 Whangpoo Road
Spain	1205 Bubbling Well Road
Sweden	96 Rue Marcel Tillot
Switzerland	113 R. de Say Zoong

Chambers of Commerce:

Information concerning business in Shanghai (so far as the country of the visitor is concerned) may be found at the local Chambers of Commerce, of which there are many represented in Shanghai.

American	51 Canton Road
Brazilian	1290 Rue Lafayette

British	17 The Bund
Chinese	N. Soochow & Honan Rds.
Danish	220 Szechuen Road
French	9 Avenue Edward VII
General	17 The Bund
German	133 Yuen Ming Yuen Road
Italian	278 Kiangse Road
Japanese	24 The Bund
Netherlands	Sassoon House
Norwegian	220 Szechuen Road

Trade Conditions.—Commercial attaches, associated with the principal Consulates, compile statistics on general trade conditions in China, possibilities for new markets, and commercial developments. They are glad to be of any possible assistance to their nationals.

The American Commercial Attache and the American Trade Commissioner have their offices, not at the U.S. Consulate, but at 51 Canton Road (Robert Dollar building), and the Canadian Trade Commissioner is at 17 The Bund. Other commercial attaches and trade commissioners are at their respective Consulates.

MUNICIPAL OFFICES

International Settlement:

Fire Brigade   309 Honan Road   Phone 15440

Police Force	239 Hankow Road	Phone 15380
Public Health	223 Hankow Road	Phone 12410
Public Library	22 Nanking Road	Phone 10404
French Concession:		
Medical Service	300 Rte. Delastre	Phone 71033
Fire Brigade	193 Ave. Joffre	Phone 80079
Police	22 Rte. Stanislas	
	Chevalier	Phone 82110

DEFENCE FORCES

Foreign defences in Shanghai are maintained by the Fourth Marines (American) of whom there are 1,900; the Second Battalion of the Worcestershire Regiment (British), to be replaced by the Inniskillings in the coming trooping season, numbering 1,600 men; the Japanese Naval Landing Party, 2,100; the French Forces, 1,600, and the Shanghai Volunteer Corps, just over 2,000.

In addition to the military forces there are usually Italian, French, American, British, and Japanese naval forces in Shanghai.

There are twenty-three units in the Shanghai Volunteer Corps, the Light Horse, American Troop, Shanghai Field Battery, Shanghai Light Battery, Shanghai Field Company, Armoured Car Company, "A" Company, "B" Company, American Company, Portuguese Company, Japanese Company, Chinese Company, Shanghai Scottish, Jewish Company, Philippine Company, American Machine Gun Company, American Reservists' Company, Transport Company, Intercommunication Company, Interpreter Company, Air Defense Company, Public School Cadet Company, and the Russian Regiment. Most of the Russian Regiment is comprised of paid men. All other units are voluntary.

Chapter Twelve
EXCURSIONS FROM SHANGHAI

USING Shanghai as a base, the traveller who is remaining for some time has the choice of many excursions to points of historic interest in Central and North China, with transportation, in most cases, available by rail, air, ocean or river. The railway service in China is government-owned, comfortable and reliable. Air and water facilities are likewise efficiently operated. Railway services mentioned are available from the North Station, Shanghai.

Railway tariffs and schedules are subject to change by official notice. It is recommended that visitors to Shanghai making excursions from this city entrust arrangements for transportation, hotel reservations, guides, etc., to one of the several reliable tourist or travel agencies. Among them are:

American Express Co.	158 Kiukiang Road.
American Lloyd	13 Edward Ezra Road.
China Travel Service	420 Szechuen Road.
Thomas Cook & Son	Nanking and Szechuen Roads.
The Travel Advisers	51 Canton Road.
Japan Tourist Bureau	86 Canton Road.

The China Travel Service arranges and supervises excursions throughout China; the Japan Tourist Bureau confines itself to Japan. Other agencies listed operate world-wide services.

Guides are always available for out-of-the-way places and native quarters and should be used. They may be retained through hotels or travel agencies. The "guides" who loiter about hotel entrances and city gates should be avoided. Usually they are not guides but "runners" for enterprising merchants.

In this chapter detailed information is given concerning Hangchow, Soochow, Wusih, Nanking, Tientsin, Peiping (Peking), Pootoo, and the Yangtsze Gorges. Railway passenger tar-

West Lake, Hangchow

iffs, where quoted, are only for first class accommodations; second and third class rates are much cheaper. All tariffs are quoted in Shanghai currency.

HANGCHOW

The capital of Chekiang Province with a population of about 400,000, Hangchow was once the site of the Forbidden City of the Southern Sung Dynasty. More than thirty centuries before Marco Polo came to add his tribute to the praises of West Lake, a populous city existed here. About 2,000 years before Christ, during the period of Yu-Kung, the place was under the jurisdiction of Yangchow (where Marco Polo afterward was magistrate under Kublai Khan). About 1,500 years later, in the time of Chun-shin, what is to-day Hangchow was called Yueh, and from then on its prestige and fame have increased and spread over China. During the Southern Sung Dynasty (1127-1280) it was probably the largest city in the world, and one of the richest. All the arts flourished here under Imperial patronage. With Sung artists came a renaissance which produced some of the most classical art and literature in China's cultural heritage.

Hangchow is the southern terminus of the Grand Canal. This great artificial inland waterway, still of vast commercial importance, is more than 900 miles in length, extending from Hangchow to Tientsin in the North. To the South of Hangchow, and spreading out in fanlike embrace behind Si-Hu, or West Lake, is a range of low mountains. Only on the North is the city unprotected by natural barriers, there being a broad level plain reaching toward Shanghai. The railway journey from Shanghai, a distance of 131 miles, is about five hours. A recently opened motor road also enables tourists to go from Shanghai to Hangchow by car.

Favoured Resort. — The temperature at Hangchow ranges between 35 and 83 degrees (Fahrenheit) but remains near 70 during most of the year, which partly accounts for its being the most favoured resort in China. Notable temples of Buddhism and Taoism, some of them of great age, have been objects of pilgrimage for many centuries. Near Hangchow are several beautiful mountain resorts, most favoured of which is Mokanshan, about 40 miles to the northwest. Mokanshan ("Isolated Peak") is a favourite Summer resort for many Shanghailanders. The mountain is 2500 feet high and the scenery and climate are compelling attractions. There are many recreational facilities. A visit to Mokanshan, especially in the hot weather period, is recommended. These attractions, and the phenomenon of the Hangchow Bore, one of the wonderful sights of the world, are some of the chief lures that bring thousands to Hangchow every year, to go away repeating the Chinese proverb, "Above there is Heaven and beneath are Hang and Soo," the last referring to Soochow. Both cities, historic and celebrated in song, have been an earthly paradise to the Chinese for more than 4,000 years.

West Lake possesses a romantic urge not to be resisted. From West Lake Marco Polo enjoyed the beauties of Hangchow. He dwelt at great length in the reports of his travels on this city, which he said was "the greatest in all the world."

Famous Monasteries. — The monasteries in the hills beyond West Lake are interesting. The more famous of these, and the pagoda temples surrounding West Lake should be visited before one leaves "Hang." Until a few years ago there stood on the southwest eminence overlooking the lake a structure of red brick, called the "Thunder Peak Pagoda," which was, built by a concubine of one of the Wu Yueh princes about 975 A.D. Within the last few decades it had crumbled until there was merely an ivy-cloaked mound of broken brick and in 1924 it suddenly collapsed into shapeless ruins. It was perhaps the most noted of the few surviving relics of other days, being approximately ten centuries old, and it is worth noting that the Hangchow Municipality is considering its restoration.

[151]

On the same hill is a Buddhist temple, one of the four largest bordering West Lake. It is called the Ziang-dz-sz, and is especially dear to Japanese Buddhists for it is supposed to be the place where the celebrated Nipponese priest and educator, Kobe Daishi, first studied the teachings of Gautama.

Cupid's Temple.—The most famous temple in which Cupid is worshipped in China is a small shrine on one of the tiny islands in the West Lake, Hangchow. It is known as "White Cloud Temple." Thousands of lovers, eager to know if their romances will last forever, and thousands of others who want to know where to go to meet their future mates, visit the shrine every year. The legendary role played by Cupid is not widely known among the Chinese. In modern Chinese wedding ceremonies Cupids are used to decorate the groom's ears. Cupid is better known as "Foreign God of Wealth." Many refuse to believe that the tiny archer could be a god of wealth as the Chinese conception of the God of Wealth is a black warrior on a black tiger. The doubters call Cupid the "God of Many Offspring." Decorating the bridal motor car with Cupids means that the newly married pair will have many sons.

General Ward's Tomb.—En route to Hangchow, and about thirty miles from Shanghai, is Sungkiang, a city which contains the tomb of Frederick Townsend Ward, the American who organized and first commanded "The Ever Victorious Army" (*see* Chapter One). An annual pilgrimage, promoted by American war veterans in Shanghai and in which many Chinese participate, is made to the tomb.

Trains for Hangchow may be taken at the North Station in Shanghai. Round trip to Hangchow, express, $13; one way $8.25. Diners are attached to the trains and tea is served in the compartments. Both foreign style and Chinese hotels are available, at reasonable rates.

THE HANGCHOW BORE

A most remarkable natural phenomenon which each year

attracts thousands of visitors to the Hangchow district, is the Hangchow Bore, the huge ram of water which sweeps up the bay and the Ch'ien T'ang river near the first and middle of every lunar month. The Bore, however, is much greater at the Spring and Autumn equinoxes and the greatest usually occurs two days after the full moon nearest the autumnal equinox, about the middle of September.

The ordinary bi-monthly bores are usually five to six feet high at the front of the thundering mass of water, while the equinoxial bores occasionally reach a height of eighteen to twenty-five feet and it is asserted that bores of more than thirty feet have been witnessed.

The formation of the bores is easily explained. Hangchow Bay is shaped like a huge funnel, sixty miles wide at the mouth and narrowing down to the Ch'ien T'ang river. One hundred miles inland the 60-mile wide funnel has narrowed to a tube only two miles wide. Incoming tides, driving into this great funnel, rise higher and higher, meet the current of the river, and the Bore is created, at its best a snowy crested solid wall of water, perhaps, at a good season, twenty feet high and travelling at fifteen to eighteen miles an hour.

The best view of the Bore is obtained at Haining, a town forty miles from Hangchow, and about twelve miles from where the Bore begins to form, at a point where the bay is narrowed to two and a half miles. The equinoxial bores are magnificent spectacles. The roar of the inrushing water may be heard for half an hour before the crest reaches Haining and for a like period after it has passed that point.

SOOCHOW

Older than the memory of Confucius, a famous city six hundred years before the birth of Christ, and, once the capital of the Kingdom of Wu — such is Soochow, a brief two-hour train ride from Shanghai. This city of canals and bridges is a real Chinese city, very slightly touched by foreign influence, a relic and a memory of the cities of Cathay as they were centuries ago.

As a famous holiday resort of China it rivals even fair Hangchow in scenic beauty and historic interest. Its greatest distinction, however, is not its scenery nor its historical background, but its beautiful women!

The most beautiful women in China (so say the Chinese) have always been found in Soochow and poems in their praise have been sung perpetually by Chinese and foreign bards. Chinese poets, for many ages past, have turned their rhymes and laid them at the dainty feet of the ladies of Soochow, and foreign rhymesters, ever since Soochow was opened to foreign trade in 1896, as a result of the Sino-Japanese war, have been following their example.

In approaching Soochow by rail one proceeds along the city wall (one of the few famous city walls left in China) which is girdled by a moat and has six gates.

There are six bridges spanning the moat. Within the wall rickshaws will be waiting to take passengers to their hotels or sightseeing.

In the main streets of the city will be found the bazaars and shops which specialize, largely, on the gorgeous silks for which Soochow is justly famous. In these bazaars silks and embroideries may be found at incredibly cheap prices.

Temples of Soochow. — In the busiest section of the city, approximately the centre, will be found the Buddhist Temple, Yuen-Miao-Kwei, the main temple of which was founded during the Tang period. It is one of the most representative relics of the Indian religion in China. The temple is a favourite resort of the people of the city and in its compound, in addition to the tea houses, variety shows, etc., are open-air stalls where numerous articles are sold. The street fronting the temple is one of the busiest in Soochow.

The Temple of Confucius is a splendid shrine surrounded by tall, ancient trees. The present buildings are new, restorations of the originals destroyed by the Taiping rebels. The Temple of Lady

Chen was founded by a general of the Kingdom of Wu and its famous pagoda was built during the Ming period, between 1583 and 1592. The pagoda is 250 feet high and one of the most stately structures South of the Yangtsze. From the ninth storey a good view of the city and its surrounding plains with their numerous lakes and canals may be obtained.

The twin pagodas of the Twin-Tower Temple were built between 984 and 994 A.D. The temple buildings were destroyed by the Taiping rebels who, however, spared these quaint and picturesque pagodas. Sze Chi-lin, near the Ping Gate, is reputed to be one of the finest gardens in the southeastern part of China.

Outside the walls of Soochow, one mile West of the Tsangmen Gate, is a typical Chinese garden, containing fine examples of miniature hills, lakes, streams, trees, flowers, herbs, bridges, and Chinese prints and antiques in pottery. It was once the villa of a Mandarin but is now owned by the wealthy heirs of a famous statesman of the later period of the Ching Dynasty. The garden is private but visitors are admitted at 10 cents per person.

The Leaning Pagoda. — Twenty minutes ride by rickshaw from West Garden is Tiger Hill, where stands the "Leaning Pagoda" of Soochow, said to be more than 1,000 years old, and as famous in China as the Pisa Tower is in Europe. It leans at about a 15 degree angle to the northwest, and is gradually slipping more.

Precious Belt Bridge, 12,000 feet long, spans a wide stream connecting the Grand Canal with Lake Tan Tai-hu, two miles southeast of the city.

Ling Yen-san, a hill on which stands a famous temple, is twelve miles northwest of the city, the two being connected by a canal. On a summit is the Lute Terrace, much revered by young men in love, for it was here that an historic beauty, Si-sz, of the court of the Kingdom of Yueh, once played a golden lute so sweetly that all the orioles of the mountain were hushed for a year after, so great was their admiration of the young woman's talent.

Soochow is 54 miles West of Shanghai on the Shanghai-Nan-

king railway line. First class round trip to Soochow, $4.95; one way, $3.30. Express trains, round trip, $6.15; one way, $3.90. Good Chinese hotels are available, serving food in both Chinese and foreign style.

WUSIH

Twenty-seven miles West of Soochow, an hour by train, is Wusih, a rapidly growing all-Chinese industrial community of great interest. Smokestacks on the skyline offer a curious contrast to the pagodas further back on the hills, symbols of a vanishing era. Wusih is progressive. From a population of less than 100,000 some twenty years ago it has become a metropolis of more than half a million. Wusih has been aptly termed the "Manchester of China."

A short distance from the city is Lake Taihu, and nearby flows the Grand Canal, linking up with all the major waterways giving exit to the sea. Before 1912 Wusih was a simple trading centre with rice and raw silk as the chief items of exchange. To-day there are ten large cotton mills, eighteen textile weaving plants, forty-five silk filatures, five flour mills, ten wood oil factories, one satin plant, two rice mills, five soap factories, two manufacturers of prepared foodstuffs, two distilleries, one paper factory, five knitting mills (hosiery), and one bean oil factory. These plants are all under Chinese ownership and operation. In addition to these are many smaller industries. Electric light and power plants and a modern telephone exchange are further evidences of the advancement of the city.

More than 150,000 workers are engaged in the industries of Wusih;

A Pailou (Memorial Arch)

for the silk filatures alone over 20,000 are required, this business now exceeding $210,000,000 annually. The value of the cocoon crop used in silk manufacture is in excess of $24,000,000 a year, while some 50,000,000 pounds of raw cotton is annually consumed by Wusih factories. Most of the cotton is domestic, although considerable quantities are imported from America.

Nor is all of the interest of Wusih confined to industrialism. Mei-Yoen, or Plum Garden, is one of the finest botanical gardens in China, covering an area of about 200 acres. Pleasure cruises may be made on Lake Taihu. Before leaving Wusih the visitor should see one of the "mud-men factories" of a curious industry that has identified itself with the city. All manner of fascinating little images are turned out, classical Mandarins, and military men, important generals of the Revolution, and famous beauties from the courts of the past. The material used is a clay found in the neighbourhood of Wusih.

Railroad fare to Wusih from Shanghai; round trip, $6.55; one way, $4.35.

NANKING

Heir to rich annals of the past, Nanking; the present seat of the National Government of China was, for six dynasties between the fourth and sixth centuries, the classical capital of South China. During the reign of the Mings it became, for a time, the national capital. The earliest of the Mings built his Forbidden City here in 1368 and it was when his successors moved North

Moon Bridge, Soochow

to Peking that the city received its present name, which means "Southern Capital." Despite its loss of political importance in early days, Nanking remained the leading cultural centre of South China and when the Ming Dynasty finally was ousted by the Manchus the latter made Nanking the chief city under a viceroyship which included the provinces of Kiangsi, Kiangsu and Anhwei. The Taipings took Nanking on March 18, 1853, killed all its Imperialist defenders, and held it for eleven years as the capital of the rebel "Kingdom of Great Peace" until the fall of the anti-imperialistic movement.

It was at Nanking that the revolutionists of 1911 set up their provisional government under the leader-ship of Dr. Sun Yat-sen. After the overthrow of the Manchus at Peking, affairs for a time were administered from this city. Later the capital was again removed to Peking until 1927 when the Cantonese came North and set up the National Government in Nanking, where it is still established.

Before the Revolution of 1911 the population of Nanking had dwindled to about 200,000 but it has since become a "boom" town. It is estimated that the present population of Greater Nanking exceeds 1,000,000 and it is rapidly growing.

The Nanking Wall is 32 miles long, varying in height from 30 to 50 feet, with supporting embankments ranging from 20 to 40 feet in width, making it one of the sturdiest surviving structures of its kind. Most of the wall is still in excellent condition, a fine example of the solid masonry that characterized edifices of the Imperial Mings.

From the shore of the Yangtsze, through Nanking, the Sun Yat-sen Road proceeds in unbroken regularity for 12 miles to the foot of the $3,000,000 Purple Mountain memorial erected as the tomb of Dr. Sun Yat-sen. A wide, well-paved boulevard, it is the first impressive evidence of virility in Nanking which greet the newly arrived. The Sun Yat-sen Memorial is three miles beyond the wall, surrounded by hills, and towering above the Ming Tombs.

Ming Tombs.—Situated at the southwest base of the Purple Mountain is the tomb of the Emperor Tai-Tsu, the founder of the Ming Dynasty, and of his consort, Ma Huang-hou. The tombs are surrounded by extensive brick walls. Many former large buildings outside the walls were destroyed by the Taiping rebels but the stone figures of men and horses along the entrance pathway, works of great skill, can still be seen to-day.

Other places of historic interest which should be visited in Nanking are Sz-Tou-Tse, where the King of Wu first built his castle and where the remains of walls and foundation stones bear witness to the hundreds of battles fought on the hill; Wu-Lung-Tang, or Black Dragon Pool, full of fish and tortoises; Ma-Tsou-

Hu, a lake famous for lotus flowers, bordered with willow trees; and Chi-Hsia-Shan Sz, a Buddhist Temple with a tower of 50 feet, in which are preserved the ashes of Emperor Wen of the Sui Dynasty. At the left of the temple is the "Hill of One Thousand Buddhas," over-grown with ancient pines, in the midst of which are 1,000 images of Buddha.

In contrast to the ancient tombs and temples are the fine new government buildings and universities. Thousands of students come from all parts of China to this great educational and cultural centre.

The trip to Nanking from Shanghai may be made by train, river steamer, or airplane. By rail, 195 miles; round trip, $19; one way, $11.85; sleeper, $4.50. The night express leaves the North Station in Shanghai at 11 p.m. and arrives at Nanking at 7 a.m.

By river, 210 miles; approximately 30 hours; round trip fare, about $48.

By air, two hours and fifteen minutes; round trip, $70; one way, $40. Airplane leaves Lunghua Field, Shanghai, at 6.30 a.m. and arrives at Nanking at 8.45.

Excellent foreign hotel accommodations are available.

TIENTSIN

Only about three hours by rail from the centuries-old city of Peiping (Peking) is one of the finest and most modern cities in China. Tientsin, 821 miles from Shanghai by rail, is the second most important port of China, with a population at this writing of more than 1,000,000.

The visitor to Tientsin will be greatly impressed by its cleanliness as contrasted with other cities of China. Even the Native City of Tientsin is almost entirely free from beggars and has broad paved streets and smart shops. Comparison of it with the Native City of Shanghai is much to the disadvantage of the latter.

The foreign concessions of Tientsin—French, Japanese, Italian and British—are clean and modern in appearance. Trees border the paved boulevards and the residential sections are more suggestive of the Occident than the Orient. Hotel accommodations are excellent and there are many fine clubs.

The important fur and rug industries of China are centered in Tientsin and remarkable bargains (judged by Occidental standards) may be obtained in these products. In the Japanese Concession there is a Curio Bazaar which is well worth a visit.

Sightseers will find numerous temples in the Native City, the most famous being the Hai Kwan Sze, with its huge bronze bell. A splendid view of the city may be had from the Drum Tower near the Li Hung-chang memorial.

Tientsin may be reached from Shanghai by train, ocean steamer or airplane. The city is located on the Hai-Ho River and steamer passengers land at Taku Bar, entering the city by train, a half-hour trip.

Steamer trip to Tientsin from Shanghai, two days; fare, $90 each way.

Railway fare, one way, $70.35, plus berth and dining expenses; round trip, $109.95.

Airplane leaves the Lunghua Field (Shanghai) at 6.30 a.m. and arrives at Tientsin at 2.45 p.m.; fare, $160 each way.

Hotel accommodations are comparable with those of Shanghai with approximately the same rates.

PEIPING (PEKING)

Peiping, one of the oldest cities in the world, and one of the most interesting! He who has not seen Peiping has really not seen the China of fable and history. Peiping, 918 miles from Shanghai by rail, dates back more than 3,000 years in recorded history. Possessed of surpassing charms, Peiping undoubtedly is one of the wonders of the world. Its historical background is gorgeously rich.

Tartars, Mongols, Mings, and Manchus have, in turn, swayed the empire of which Peiping for so long was the keystone. The height of royal magnificence was attained from 1200 to 1300 A.D. during the reign of the great Kublai Khan, the glories of whose court were recounted by the Venetian explorer, Marco Polo.

Although much of its grandeur has departed since the removal of the Chinese capital to Nanking, Peiping yet remains a city of romance and charm. From its lofty walls, thirty miles in circumference and enclosing an area of twenty square miles, the golden tiled roofs of the Tartar and Chinese cities gleam in symbolism of the immeasurable wealth they shelter. Palaces decorated with grotesque gargoyles record the reigns of otherwise forgotten Emperors. And, as in centuries past, the camel caravans leave the Imperial City for the lands of mystery to the North and West.

Peiping is a city of walls. Private homes, the legations, and public buildings are surrounded by walls, all sheltered by the tremendous wall which girdles the entire city.

Peiping is in the same latitude as southern Italy, but it has a wide seasonal range of climate, cold winters and hot summers.

Legation Quarter. — Peaceful and quiet, as distinguished from the turmoil of other sections, and surrounded by its wall, the Legation Quarter contains the official headquarters of thirteen nations, American, Belgian, British, Brazilian, Danish, French, German, Italian, Japanese, Netherlands, Portuguese, Spanish, and Russian. The legation buildings are palatial, with beautiful gardens. As each nation has followed its own style of architecture, the appearance of the Quarter is somewhat startling, but pleasing. The streets are broad and paved and tree-lined. The Quarter has its own shopping and business section.

It was in the Legation Quarter that the foreigners of Peking made their last desperate stand against the Chinese during the Boxer uprising in 1900, holding out until relieved by the allied forces.

Dr. Sun Yat-sen's Mausoleum, Nanking

Other points of interest in Peiping will be touched upon briefly, but with little attempt at definite locations and directions, as guides are urgently advised for the tour of Peiping and environs. Reputable agencies such as Thomas Cook & Son and the American Express Co. can make all necessary arrangements.

Forbidden City.—For many years the Forbidden City was a complete and engaging mystery to the Occident, for foreigners were not admitted to its sacred precincts until after the Boxer uprising in 1900. It is, perhaps, the most famous of all the walled cities within Peiping. Despite looting and spoliation, much of the grandeur of this Imperial City remains. The present palaces date from the Ming dynasty and occupy, roughly, the site of the court of Kublai Khan, 1214-1294, the Grand Khan of the Mongols, who conquered China and founded the Yuen dynasty, making Buddhism the state religion. He was the heroic figure made immortal by Marco Polo.

The Museum section of the Forbidden City is composed of

[164]

fifteen buildings, and here once were stored the most remarkable art collections in all China. During the Sino-Japanese troubles of 1932 thousands of cases of these priceless treasures were shipped out to Nanking and Shanghai for safekeeping. Their return is still an open question. Much of interest, however, remains to be seen within the fabled Forbidden City. The jade and bronze collections are beyond question the finest in the world.

Summer Palace.—Once a place of indescribable grandeur, the Summer Palace, some seven miles out from the Tartar City of Peiping, a favourite resort of the old Empress Dowager, who was responsible for its construction, is still well worth the time required for a visit. There is a haunting beauty in the temples, palaces, shrines and pagodas. The land- and water-scaping are particularly effective.

Some of the more modern buildings and the famous marble boat were the work of the Empress Tz'u Hsi, who used for the purpose $30,000,000 which had been appropriated for the construction of a Chinese Navy. To this circumstance some historians have attributed the defeat of China by Japan in the war of 1894. The war was lost but the marble boat remains.

Three miles West of the Summer Palace is the Jade Fountain, a spring which has been giving forth water for countless centuries. It supplies the lakes of the Summer Palace grounds. The park at the fountain is beautiful and there are interesting pagodas in the adjacent hills.

Winter Palace.—Within Peiping there is no more beautiful spot than the grounds of the Winter Palace, in which are included the group known as the Sea Palaces. There are many pavilions and two attractive lakes, separated by a marble bridge. In Autumn the lakes are almost covered with lotus blooms. Boat picnics on the lakes are a favourite summer-time diversion.

Don't fail to see the Nine Dragon Screen at the Winter Palace, one of the most famous art treasures of the city. The colourings of the porcelains are exquisite and the entire screen is intact.

The White Jade Buddha, enshrined in a small temple to the

Nanking Park

left of the large entrance of the Winter Palace, is decidedly worth inspection. The Round City, in which this huge Buddha is to be found, was once the principal residence of Kublai Khan, and the temple which it occupies was the site of his throne room. Most of the palaces are constructed of tile decorated in the famous imperial yellow and in green, the colours having remained vivid and distinct throughout the centuries. In fact, throughout Peiping, one gains a lasting impression of changeless age.

Temple of Heaven. — Located in the Chinese City are the famous Temple of Heaven and the Altar of Agriculture. The temple grounds are interesting and are surrounded by a wall more than three miles in circumference. This was long the imperial shrine where the Emperors made their addresses to the gods of ancient China. Five temples really form the group collectively known as the Temple of Heaven.

The Altar of Heaven, long regarded as the most sacred place in China, is a huge marble platform with three terraces and 360 balustrades. The first terrace is 210 feet in width. Many visitors have adjudged the Temple of Heaven the most impressive of Peiping's many scenic attractions.

Lama Temple.—This famous temple, one of the fountain heads of Lamaism, a decadent branch of Buddhism, with much obscenity in the ritual, is in reality a monastery, wherein reside about 1,500 priests. The chanting of the priests, in their bizarre costumes, is a most unusual spectacle. The Passion Buddhas, in ribald postures, ostensibly concealed, may be seen—for a price in tips.

A most interesting object is an immense image of the Buddhist redeemer, Maitreya, seventy feet high and said to have been carved from a single tree trunk. A winding stairway affords a close-up view of this striking figure. There is a huge praying wheel in the same building. The Lama Temple, buildings and tree-shaded grounds, offer much else of interest to the visitor.

Temple of Agriculture. — Dedicated to Shen Nung, said to have ruled China some three thousand years before the Christian era and who is credited with the invention of the plow, this temple has been modernized until to-day it is largely a pleasure park. It is located across the avenue from the Temple of Heaven.

Within the spacious grounds are Chinese theatres, restaurants, tea houses and many recreational facilities. It is a very popular resort for the Chinese. Well worth a visit for a glimpse of native life in holiday spirit.

Drum and Bell Towers. — Attaining a height of 130 feet, the Drum Tower gives one a splendid view of the Tartar City. It is a landmark of Peiping.

The Bell Tower, same height as the Drum Tower, contains the great bell cast at the order of the Emperor Yung-lo. Legend has it that the Emperor, infuriated by several unsuccessful attempts to produce a perfect bell, proclaimed that another failure would doom the chief artisan to death. The latter's beautiful daughter, when the next effort was made, leaped into the molten metal and perished. The bell was perfect. It is a Chinese legend that the maiden's sighs are the minor notes of the bell's chimes.

Observatory. — The oldest astronomical observatory in the world is located in Peiping, having first been built by Kublai Khan in 1279. The ancient Chinese were well versed in astrology when it was an unknown science in Europe. Many of the old instruments may yet be seen, but most of the finer pieces were lost to the Germans when the allied troops looted the city during the Boxer fighting in 1900.

Temple of 10,000 Punishments. — A Taoist temple, illustrating with painted wooden figures the ingenuity of the ancient Chinese in devising forms of torture. Taoists suffering from ill health utilize it as a shrine at which to pray for relief. It is a large building, with interesting courtyards.

Marco Polo Bridge. — Spanning the Hun Ho river, this remarkable stone structure of thirty-five arches still stands after more than a thousand years as a monument to the sound workmanship

Temple of Heaven, Peiping

of Chinese engineers. It is now named for the Venetian explorer who said it was the most wonderful bridge he had ever seen.

Eunuchs' Cemetery. — A half-hour motor trip from the city brings one to the Eunuchs' Cemetery, where for centuries the favourite eunuchs of the Emperors were buried. There are hundreds of tombs, many of them large and imposing. The spacious, forested grounds are beautiful.

Shopping. — Peiping is a veritable paradise for the curio hunter, as well as for those who fancy rugs, embroideries, tapestries, old jewellery, bronzes, etc. Beware of unscrupulous dealers. It is safer, and usually far more profitable, to patronize the well-established foreign shops or those reputable native merchants who are well known, recommended and legitimately advertised.

Excursions From Peiping.—From Peiping three major side excursions are recommended; to the Western Hills, the Ming Tombs, and the Great Wall.

WESTERN HILLS

The first near view of the Western Hills is obtained from Pa Ta Ch'u, about forty minutes from Peiping by motor. Donkeys and chairs may be engaged for the ascent of the hills to the temples and other points of interest.

The temples which dot the Western Hills date from the Ming period in the fifteenth century, some of them even antedating that era. The scenery is magnificent, and ancient temples, shrines, monasteries, tombs, etc., are to be found on every side.

One of the main centres of attraction is the "Mummy Temple." Shun Chih, first of the Manchu Emperors, is said to have died in a cave near a monastery where he retired from the world upon refusal of the court to allow him to wed a favourite concubine. His body was mummified and further preserved with bronzed lacquer. He sits in eternal meditation over his lost love in the centre of an ornate temple.

Other points of outstanding interest in the Western Hills are the famous Trappist Monastery and the Black Dragon Pool and Temple. If time is available the guides will take one to many other points well worth inspection.

MING TOMBS

A motor car is recommended for the visit to the Ming Tombs, twenty-five miles northwest of Peiping, for, if made by train, donkeys must be taken at Nankow for the remaining ten miles to the Tombs. Food and water should be carried for this one-day excursion.

The Tombs are in a rugged country, surrounded by beautiful mountain scenery. They are widely separated and if many of them are to be seen the tour must be made on donkeys, as there are no connecting roads.

The oldest and largest tomb, and the one most frequently visited as it is also the most accessible, is that of Yung Loh, who died in 1425, and who was responsible for the building of much of Peiping.

One of the great attractions is the gigantic Ancestral Hall, 80 by 180 feet. The roof is supported by forty pillars of solid tree trunks, fifty feet high and a yard in diameter. In the courtyard beyond the Hall will be found a huge sacrificial table of carved marble.

In approaching the Ming Tombs one encounters a magnificent gate, declared by many to be the finest in China. It is featured by five arches of elaborately carved marble, four pillars, and a tiled roof.

GREAT WALL

The journey to the Great Wall of China is made by train, leaving Peiping in the morning and returning the same day. If a more extensive inspection is desired, a stopover may be made.

There is nothing new to be said about the Great Wall. Most school boys are familiar with the broad outlines of its history. However, it is indubitably one of the wonders of the world, perhaps the most stupendous physical creation of mankind. More than two thousand years old and fifteen hundred miles long, this tremendous barrier of masonry sweeps across mountain and over dale with a majestic defiance of natural obstacles. No one who can see it should miss doing so.

The height of the wall ranges from twenty to fifty feet, it is from fifteen to twenty-five feet wide at the base and at the top averages twelve feet. Lofty watch towers rise from the level of the wall at intervals. For many years the Great Wall was the greatest trade route between the Chinese and the northern Tartars. Even to-day camel caravans travel along the wall.

Transportation to Peiping.—Peiping may be reached from Shanghai by railway or by airplane, or even by ocean steamer to Taku (Tientsin) and thence by train. (*See* Tientsin section).

The Great Wall of China

By the Shanghai-Peiping through express train one way fare, $76.95, plus berth and dining car expenses; round trip, $120.35.

By air, leave Lunghua Field (Shanghai) at 6:30 a.m., arrive at Peiping at 3.30 p.m. One way, $180; round trip, $300.

Excellent hotel accommodations, at moderate rates, are available in Peiping.

"HOLY LAND" OF CHINA

As Jerusalem is to the Christians, and Mecca to the Mohammedans, so is Chufou to the Confucians of China. The Province of Shantung is the "Holy Land" of China and it was here, in the village of Chufou, that Confucius (551-478 B.C.) was born, lived, and died. Not far from the tiny village is the sacred mountain Tai Shan, one of the most venerated of China's five sacred mountains. It is said to be the oldest place of worship in the world.

Travellers by rail between Peiping and Shanghai pass through the historic cities of Shantung and a stopover at a few of them will add infinitely to a knowledge and understanding of China. Chufou, birthplace of Confucius; Tsowhsien, where Mencius, a celebrated sage and philosopher and disciple of Confucius was born; and Taianfu, behind which the Jade Emperor, chief god of the Taoist triad and ruler of every mountain top, rules over the summit of Tai Shan, are the triumvirate which compose the holy centre of China.

Chufou, birthplace of Confucius, only a little more than 500 miles from Shanghai, is unquestionably one of the most interesting villages in China. Picturesque and ancient, scarcely anything has changed here since 551 B.C. when the Sage was born. Of particular interest is the Grand Hall of Ceremonial Practice, built entirely of carved wood. At Spring and Autumn festivals each year millions of Chinese make pilgrimages to this Hall to pay homage to Confucius. The Main Hall of the Temple of Confucius is one of the finest examples of Chinese temple architecture in existence. It is 74 feet high and has double curled roofs of emerald tile, with marble pillars supporting the giant edifice. Deeply carved single slabs of stone are exquisitely artistic. Within the Hall is a famous statue of Confucius with other statues and portraits of his disciples. Many of these works are of great value. Outside the Hall is the well from which Confucius drank and the Pagoda Tree which he is said to have planted. An avenue, lined with ancient cypress trees and flanked by monstrous stone dragons, lions, unicorns, and horses leads to a park.

Ancient Worship. — Fifty miles north of Chufou is Taianfu, at the base of Tai Shan, or "Eastern Peak of Heaven." At the railroad station chairs may be hired for the ascent. Men worshipped at Tai Shan long before the Greeks sanctified Olympus or built the Temple of Athena. Tai Shan was sacred in China centuries before Fujiyama was sacred in Japan, and long before Moses received the Ten Commandments on Mount Sinai. It has been sacred for at least 4,000 years. Tai Shan is the tallest peak in the Kuenluen mountain range, 6,000 feet high. A wide stone stairway, "The Road to Heaven," has 6,500 steps and starts the climb to the peak. On the way there are gates, temples and shrines — The First Gate of Heaven, the Red Gate Palace, the Tower of the Goddess of Mercy, etc. It takes from four to five hours to reach the South Gate of Heaven, where the climb is over. The Confucian temple here was erected in the sixteenth century.

About two hours north of Taianfu, by train, is Tsinanfu, capital of the province and a modern city with wide paved streets, factories, electric lighting, parks, department stores, etc. Visitors interested in Christian work in China will find many missionary institutions here, and the Shantung Christian University. Near Tsinanfu, en route to Tientsin, one crosses the Yellow River over a bridge built by Germans at a cost of $5,000,000. It is 4,116 feet long and is one of the most difficult engineering works yet undertaken in the Far East.

Travellers to China's Holy Land may start from Shanghai, Peiping, or Tsingtao. From Shanghai the railroad fare to Chufou is $42; round trip, $66.15. About five dollars more is added to prolong the journey to Taianfu, and five more to Tsinanfu.

YANGTSZE GORGES

One easily drifts into superlatives in describing the scenic attractions of China. There are so many "greatest," "oldest," "largest" and "world wonders" that the phrases become trite through repetition.

No word-picture can adequately bring visualization of the grandeur and glory of the Yangtsze Gorges. They have been compared to the Grand Canyon of the Colorado, but these two great natural wonders have many points of difference, notably the fact that the Yangtsze Gorges are navigable by high-speed steamers.

Because of their isolation, few casual visitors to Shanghai make the voyage through the Yangtsze Gorges. Those who can afford the time and money should see them.

Going inland, the Gorges begin shortly beyond Ichang, approximately 1,000 miles from the sea, where the elevation is only 130 feet above sea level. In the next 400 miles, to Chungking, there is an elevation above sea level to 630 feet. Over this 400-mile stretch the mighty Yangtsze crashes through the backbone of the Asiatic continent, irresistibly carving its way to the sea in a deep channel which sunders a mountain range. Nowhere else in the world is there anything quite comparable with the Yangtsze Gorges. They must be seen to be appreciated.

The Gorges may be seen by steamer or from the air. The best season for the steamer trip is from May to November. By steamer the round trip from Shanghai to Chungking requires about three weeks, the fare averaging $400. Transportation is available from several steamship companies.

The Gorges can also be viewed from the air, the airplane trip from Shanghai to Chungking and return requiring four days; round trip fare by air, $780. The cities of Ichang and Chungking both possess many points of interest.

ISLAND OF POOTOO

The sacred island of Pootoo is fifty miles East of Ningpo (Ningpo is 150 miles South of Shanghai) and is the nearest bathing beach to Shanghai. Pootoo is a hill, from which one of the most important Buddhist gods looks down upon the world.

Gorges: Between Ichang and Wanhsien

There are about a hundred temples and monasteries, the latter being the residences of some 1,000 monks. The island is the most sacred spot to Chinese Buddhists in Eastern China and, on the alleged birthday of Kwan Yin, the goddess of mercy (19th day of 11th month of the old Chinese calendar) special stately ceremonies take place in Pootoo to which thousands of monks and laymen from all parts of China make pilgrimages.

During the Summer, from June 1 to the end of September, steamers of the China Merchants' Steam Navigation Co. run direct from Shanghai to Pootoo, enabling one to spend the weekend there. Round trip $40. The Sacred Island has no hotel, but visitors lodge in the temples and monasteries. As the island is purely Buddhist no animal meat is available but eggs and chickens may be obtained from a Chinese hospital which operates in the belief that all foreigners and non-Buddhists are ill and need such nourishment. It is advised that visitors to the island take tinned foods and their own bedding.

It is but recently that foreigners have come to appreciate the

natural beauties of Pootoo with its excellent roads and hundreds of shrines and grottos. Each monastery is a triumph of Chinese architecture and contains treasures which have accumulated for many centuries.

Provinces.—There are 18 provinces of China proper, Shantung, Kiangsu, and Chekiang being the most populous with a density of from 380 to 460 a square mile. Next come Honan, Hupeh, Anhui, Hunan, Kwangtung, Szechuen, Kiangsi, Chihli, and Fukien, with a density of population ranging from 200 to 300 per square mile. Kweichow and Shansi have an average of about 130. The most sparsely populated provinces are Shensi, Kwangsi, Yunnan and Kansu, where the density is from 30 to 90 per square mile.

*   *   *

When Shanghai was opened as a Treaty Port, "open land" was valued at 15,000 to 30,000 cash per mow.

Chapter Thirteen
GODS – LEGENDS – SUPERSTITIONS

L IKE all ancient countries – and the Chinese civilization is one of the oldest in the world – China possesses a literature gorgeously rich in legendary and mythological lore. It also has its share of curious superstitions. Space limitations prohibit anything approaching a full presentation, but in this chapter some of the most important points are touched upon.

GODS OF CHINA

Confucianism is asserted to be the religion of the learned. It is, in reality, more than a religion inasmuch as it embraces education, letters, ethics, and political philosophy. In its usual conception the term "Confucianism" means "a gentleman and a scholar." Confucius is really not a god although he has been worshipped as such for centuries.

Confucianism includes in its circle of deities the gods worshipped by the literati. Wen Ch'ang is the God of Literature. He is worshipped in most of the native schools, and pregnant women hang his picture in front of their beds so that their offspring will be scholars. Wen Ch'ang is always depicted with four other figures. He is clothed in blue and holds a sceptre in his left hand. Two of his attendants are deaf and dumb so that they cannot divulge the secrets of their master's administration as he distributes literary and intellectual gifts. One of the servants helps to distribute literary degrees. The fourth attendant is known as "Mr. Red Coat" and is a great favourite on earth as he is a protector of weak candidates for literary honours and sometimes gets them passed by merely nodding his head.

Another patron deity of literature is the God of War, one of the most popular gods of China. He is not a typical war god but averts war whenever possible and protects the people of China from its horrors. Temples in his honour are to be seen in all parts of the country. His worship is by no means confined to the officials and the army, for many trades and professions have elected him as patron saint. In former days the sword of the public executioner was kept within the temple of the God of War and, after the offending head was chopped off, the executioner tarried there to worship, knowing that the offended ghost of the headless victim would not dare to follow him home if the God of War were on the side of the executioner.

Buddhism. — The mythology of Buddhism has taken an important place in Chinese culture for almost two thousand years, since it was introduced into China in 65 A.D. As Buddha was a man who later became a god the religion originated in ancestor worship. It is based on the simple theory that when a man dies he reappears in some form or other. The legend of Buddha belongs rather to Indian that to Chinese mythology.

Goddess of Mercy. — As the Virgin Mary is the guiding spirit of Catholicism, so is Kwan Yin of the Buddhist faith. The name means, "one who notices and hears the cry of the world." Legend has it that when Kwan Yin was about to enter Heaven after her death, she heard a cry of anguish from the earth which she had just left and paused, in pity, as she was about to cross the threshold to Paradise. At first Kwan Yin was represented as a man but since the T'ang Dynasty, 618 A.D., a woman has more aptly filled the role.

Kwan Yin is adored by all, especially women and children. In almost every Temple of China there is a chapel for Kwan Yin and in thousands

A Mendicant Priest

of homes in China images of the Goddess are enshrined. As the patron Goddess of mothers she occupies an honoured position in all families. She protects in sorrow, saves the sailor in times of storm, and brings rain in time of drought. All other gods of China are feared as much as they are reverenced but Kwan Yin is beloved as a mother to all. Her throne is upon the Island of Pootoo (two days distant from Shanghai by boat) where she arrived floating on a water lily.

Taoism.—The trinity of Taoism consists of three Supreme Gods, each in a separate Heaven. The three Heavens were formed from the three airs, which are the subdivisions of the one primordial air. The first God is the source of all truth, the second God is the custodian of the sacred books and also calculates time, dividing it into epochs. The third God is the teacher of kings and emperors and the reformer of successive generations. Connected with Taoism, but not exclusively associated with it, is the worship of the Three Causes; Heaven, Earth, and Water. They are the sources of happiness, forgiveness of sins, and deliverance of evil.

Kitchen God.—The Kitchen God is a Taoist invention, but is worshipped universally by all families in China. Over sixty million pictures of him are prayed to twice a month. at new and full moon.

The God of Riches is worshipped everywhere in China and there are countless images and portraits of him. He is represented as a visitor accompanied by numerous attendants carrying all the treasures that men, women and children could possibly desire.

The God of Longevity is a domestic deity, of happy countenance with a very high forehead. He rides a stag and has a flying bat above his head. He holds in his hands a peach and a gourd and scroll are attached to his staff. The stag and bat indicate happiness while the peach, gourd, and scroll are symbols of a ripe old age.

Polytheism.—The names of the Gods of China are legion, and it would be impossible to name, much less to discuss, them all. There are Gods and Goddesses of wind, rain, snow, frost, oxen, horses, trees, flowers, rivers, tides, theatres, dogs, pigs, sheep, goats, locusts, snakes, gold, tea, salt, lamps, gems, wells, tailors, barbers, carpenters, masons, jugglers, street-walkers, wine, monkeys, lice, fire crackers, fornication, revenge, midwives, brothels, combs, innkeepers, gamblers, oculists, smallpox, liver complaint, stomach ache, Punch and Judy, butchers, bakers, candle-stick makers, shoes, ships, sealing wax, cabbage, jewellers, canaries, seed, goldfish, stallions, cobblers, chemists, strolling singers, fortune tellers, etc., etc. Not only is there a God of the eye, but there is a God of the Light of the eye. There is a special deity for smallpox and another special deity for the pock-marks which the smallpox leaves.

LEGENDS

Ministry of Thunder and Storm.—Affairs in the "Other World" of China are managed by official Bureaux or Ministries. First in importance is the Ministry of Thunder and Storms. An assortment of officials make up this body, the principal ones being Lei Tsu, the Ancestor of Thunder; Lei Kung, the Duke of Thunder; Tien Mu, the Mother of Lightning; Feng Po, the Count of Wind; and Yu Shih, the Master of Rain.

The President of the Ministry of Thunder has three eyes, one in the centre of his forehead. A ray of white light extends from the centre eye for a distance of two feet. Mounted on a black unicorn he covers millions of miles in the twinkling of an eye. The Duke of Thunder is an ugly, black, bat-winged demon with a monkey's head, claws, and an eagle's beak. The noise of thunder is produced when the Duke beats drums with a chisel and hammer which he carries with him. The Mother of Lightning wears a gorgeous robe of blue, green, red, and white. In both hands she holds a mirror from which emerge two broad streams of light. The Count of Wind is an old man with a white beard, yellow cloak, and blue and red cap. He holds a large sack and with it directs the wind which comes from his mouth in any direction it pleases him. The Master of Rain wears yellow scale-armour with a blue hat and yellow plume. He stands on a cloud and pours rain upon the earth from a watering can.

Water Dragons. — In China the Dragon controls the prosperity and peace of the country. He decides about the harvest and can make the Master of Rain pour water upon the earth if he so desires. Mountain dragons are harmful while those of lakes and rivers are friendly and helpful. Dragons differ in appearance but usually have the head of a horse, the tail of a snake, and wings. They have four legs. The imperial dragon has five claws on each foot while ordinary dragons have but four. The horns resemble those of a deer, eyes those of a devil, the claws those of an eagle while the soles of the feet are like those of a tiger. Some have ox-like ears while others hear through their horns.

The small dragon is like a caterpillar while the large dragon fills Heaven and Earth. Suspended from the neck of the dragon is a pearl which represents the sun. He has the power of transformation and may be visible or invisible at will. In the Spring

Willow Pattern Tea House, Chinese City

he ascends to the skies but in Autumn prefers the water. Some have no wings and rise in the air simply because they are dragons. A celestial dragon guards the mansions of the gods and supports them so that they do not fall. The earth dragon marks out the courses of rivers and streams while the dragon of the hidden treasures watches over the wealth concealed from mortals.

Sometimes mere mortals can actually see a dragon. If you see a cloud floating about with a curious configuration or a serpentine tail it is a dragon. The Sea-dragon kings, however, bury themselves in gorgeous palaces in the depths of the sea where they feed on opals and pearls. There are five Sea-dragon monarchs, all immortal. Their palaces, of multi-coloured transparent stones with doors of crystal, have often been seen early in the morning by persons gazing into deep waters.

The disposition of a dragon can always be determined by his colour (just in case you happen to meet with one). The blue dragon is the most compassionate. A red dragon will bestow his blessings upon you and you will have good luck during your visit to China. A yellow dragon will hear all petitions and grant wishes.

Ministry of Fire.—The Celestial organization of Fire is presided over by a President, Lo Hsuan, and five subordinate ministers. The President has a face the colour of ripe fruit of the jujube-tree, red hair and beard, and three eyes. He wears a red cloak and his horse snorts flame from his nostrils while fire darts from his hoofs.

Ministry of Epidemics.—The Ministry of Epidemics is made up of a President, Lu Yueh, and four disciples. The President wears a red garment, has a blue face, red hair, long teeth, and three eyes. In his many hands he holds a celestial seal, plague microbes, the flag of plague, and the plague sword.

Star Worship.—The star deities are adored by parents on behalf of their children. They control courtship and marriage, bring prosperity or adversity in business, send war, regulate drought, and command angels and demons. Every event in life is determined by a star ruler. In case of sickness in the family ten paper star gods are lined up, five good on one side, five bad on the other, and a feast placed before them. When the bad star gods have eaten enough they fly away and then prayers to the good star gods are offered, they listening without interference from the bad ones. The Star of Pleasure decides on betrothals, binding with silver cords the feet of those destined to become lovers. The Bone-piercing Star produces rheumatism. Fathers or mothers are killed during the year if the Morning Star is not worshipped. The Pear-Blossom Star controls lunacy, the Three-corpse Star suicide, and the Balustrade Star lawsuits.

Myth of Time.—T'ai Sui is the celestial spirit who presides over the year. He is the President of the Ministry of Time and is greatly feared by all. Whoever offends him is certain to be destroyed and he strikes when least expected. In order to avert calamities T'ai Sui is worshipped extensively for he may injure rich and poor alike at any time and at any place. He has one peculiarity which makes prevention of disaster easier. He does not injure persons in the district where he happens to be but in the adjoining district. Thus precautions may be taken by neighbouring areas if he is located in one. This is done by an elaborate diagram which verifies his geographical position.

SUPERSTITIONS

Superstitions among the uneducated Chinese run rampant from babyhood to old age and beyond. Superstitions concerning the dead are as multiple as they are of the quick. Evidences adorning the younger generation, every fetish at which the tourist stops to marvel, have roots so fundamental in Chinese tradition that they live on, presumably forever.

You will see them about the streets, children wearing padlocks attached to the neck with a silver band or chain. They are intended to chain them to existence and the padlocks keep the youngsters from being taken by death. These padlocks may be found in all silversmith shops, in all sizes and shapes.

The silver collars look like dog collars and the idea originally was taken from a dog collar. Chinese dogs live discouragingly long lives and are very healthy. It is the idea of the parent to put a collar around a child's neck so that he will do likewise. The circlet also hems in life and prevents the soul from deserting the body.

Earrings and Spirits.—Little girls wear two earrings, little boys one. Evil spirits cannot be bothered about mere girl babies and for that reason the boys are also made to wear the feminine ornament. The general idea is that evil spirits, seeing the earring, will believe that the child is a girl and go away, disgusted.

No explanation is offered as to why if one earring is effective two wouldn't be better. They are shaped like the weights of clocks, thereby giving the impression that they are heavy and hard to raise. Evil spirits are notoriously lazy and no spirit is going to bother about taking a child along who has a clock weight attached to one ear. Sometimes boy babies are even given girls' names to delude the evil spirits. The name, plus the earring, makes the boy reasonably safe.

The single strand of hair which you will see dangling down the forehead from an otherwise shaved head of a Chinese child, is not merely the Chinese idea of tonsorial pulchritude. If the lock is shorn the child is thereby exposed to an untimely death. According to stories told by the Taoist priests a youngster has to pass many barriers along the roadway of youth and if that lock of hair is missing when he arrives at the road of life the road is promptly barred and the child dies. Fortune tellers, with their rigmarole of cycles and dates, determine just when the lock may be cut off.

Engagements.—Getting engaged in old style Chinese fashion involves more red tape than a League of Nations agreement. Principals in the drama play small parts, merely following the dictates of superstitious custom. The heavy role is played by the matchmaker who tours from one family to another making overtures, agreeing upon purchase price and dowry, and getting the contract signed. Enters the fortune teller. He takes the card upon which the prospective bridegroom has written the cyclic characters indicating year of his birth, day, and hour, and a similar one made out by the bride-to-be. From this information he figures out whether the destiny of the one corresponds to the destiny of the other. This he does by comparing the characters with the five elements: metal, wood, water, fire and earth. Then he compares the two cyclic animals which have presided over the births of the parties interested, in order to ascertain whether they will abide together in harmony. The decision is based on the liking or disliking of the cyclic animals for each other. For example, the tiger is the sworn enemy of the serpent. Compatibility of elements is also determined. For instance, fire never did like water.

The lucky day for the wedding is fixed by the aid of the calendar which is carefully marked in black and yellow. Yellow is lucky, black unlucky. Another document is made out by the fortune teller and given (for a price) to the matchmaker. This fixes the day on which the wedding will take place and is sent by the young man to the family of his future bride. A third document attests that an engagement has actually taken place and is accompanied by presents. A contract is again drawn up, the young man sending his agreement to the parents of the young lady. Along with it he sends a certain sum of money, the amount being fixed by the matchmaker. There is also an assortment of knick knacks such as hair pins, earrings, rings, bracelets, and jewels, according to the standing of the parties. The bride-to-be begins to have a good time. Her family also prepares a betrothal agreement, drawn up almost on the same terms as that of the future bridegroom, and sends it to his family.

Here Comes the Bride. — After the girl has been duly informed that she is to become Mrs. So-and-so, her family again visits the fortune teller to determine the month in which she may be married in safety, the day already having been determined by the combined efforts of fortune teller and matchmaker. This is determined by the animal who presided over the month in which she first saw the

Cake Seller

light of day. For instance, if it was a hog, wedding bells (fire-crackers, to be exact) must sound in the third month. If it was a monkey the young lady is doomed to be married in the eighth month. Her fiancee does the same thing and sends his information around with more presents in a red box. The bride's family sends back a collection including herbs which will destroy evil spirits, flowers which portend riches, and vegetables which will insure numerous progeny.

The highly agitated young man finally gets around to chartering a sedan chair and goes to fetch his lady. Before stepping into his chariot he makes obeisances to all his family, the household gods, all the neighbours, and all the neighbours' household gods. A boy child must also be put into the sedan chair. After calling for his fiancee she accompanies him in another sedan chair. Before he returns her family gives him a pair of chopsticks and a couple of wine cups. These are supposed to bring cheer to the future household. Both the sedans are turned in the direction of the God of Joy while the presentation is going on, said direction having been determined by a guide chart. Sometimes the young lady's feet are padlocked. In the back of her chair there dangles a sieve and a mirror. Another mirror is attached to the bridal gown of the bride-to-be with which she does not part until she is seated on the nuptial bed. There are, of course, female attendants, equivalents of the Occidental bridesmaids and maids-of-honour. Before they are chosen they also are submitted to a fortune teller who determines if their respective cyclic animals are in harmony with the bride's.

Goddess of Fecundity.—The first wish of Chinese newlyweds is to have children. In every temple in every village in China there is a "wantchee baby" altar where earnest entreaties and offerings are laid daily. Kwan-yin is the most efficient Goddess to address on this score. A small shoe is usually offered and around any Kwan-yin shrine may always be found a number of shoes which, for some unknown reason, are never stolen. Presumably even the thieves of China respect the baby business. The shoe has to be a borrowed one, otherwise it won't work, and should the blessed event be forth-coming the shoe is returned to the original owner after the birth, together with a new pair of shoes. The Goddess of Fecundity obtains her little souls from the God of Hades, souls resurrected from Hell, and pours the souls into bodies.

In addition to Kwan-yin, numerous gods are also invoked. The God of Literature is one. Some families don't care whether their children grow up to wear spectacles and impress people or not. In that case the God of Literature is ignored. But families of official standing and the literati persistently entreat this god to bless them with his favours. A drawing of the God is hung in the nuptial chamber. In his arms he holds a child wearing an official academic headdress. The youthful descendant is not actually expected to put in his appearance in such a garb, but the general idea is that the sooner he gets into it the better.

There are numerous other pictures of a suggestive nature which immediately surround the young bride, and continue to surround her until her child-bearing days are over. Every Chinese home where there are young married people is adorned by a resplendent painted phoenix carrying an infant in its bill and headed in the general direction of the bride. There is one popular picture of the hundred children, all males of course, who share among their hundred selves all the honours and dignities of the world.

Diplomatic Fortune Teller.—When a Chinese baby is about to put in his appearance a fortune teller is consulted in regard to the sex of the child. He usually predicts that it will be a boy so as not to incur the displeasure of the future parents. A few days previous to the birth the potential mother carries a mirror around to ward off evil spirits. Many prayers are said, mostly to Buddha, to whom it is promised that the progeny will become a monk, should it be a boy. Of course he can be ransomed later on, if a few offerings are made. The practical side of the bargain is never forgotten.

After the child is born it has to wait three days before getting a bath, but on the third day it is cleansed and the fortune teller is once more summoned to cast the infant's horoscope. By that horoscope its parents are guided all through the baby's young years. Then begins the battle with the evil spirits which surround the child. Peach wood amulets are made which are either put over the "cradle" or shot into the air by archers who believe they are puncturing the evil spirits thereby. The new mother shouts curses at the devil and hires watchmen to guard the premises day and night with knives.

Neither mother nor child can leave the house, even cross the threshold, for a month after birth. Before they do go out the baby's head is shaved and the hair mixed with dog hair, which is rolled into a ball and sewn on the child's clothing. Henceforth the neighbours have nothing to fear from his presence in their homes. Copper cash is also sprung on a string and hung around a god's neck to charm away evil spirits. Later on the necklace is retrieved and put around the baby's neck. When babies learn to walk bells are tied on the little toes to frighten away hovering bad spirits.

Many people in Shanghai have, at some time or other, been presented with scarlet colored hard boiled eggs by a grinning servant who proudly announces that he has "catchee one piecee boy baby." Red is the Chinese colour of joy and it is also a lucky omen. When the babies are old enough to be taken out into the streets they may be seen with dabs of gory red on their wee noses and cheeks and foreheads.

Extreme Unction. — Dying in proper style is almost as ceremonious as getting married or being born. As soon as it becomes fairly apparent that there is to be a death in the household the relatives of the sufferer pray to summon back the soul. Half a dozen men are sent to the nearest Temple to bring a god, which is placed on a portable altar-chair to which is attached two long poles. Four men carry the chair by putting the poles over their shoulders. They chant like coolies as they walk along with their celestial burden. The other two men precede the chair, beating gongs heartily. This is to warn people along the route that the god is passing and to pay him due homage. Quantities of firecrackers are exploded along the way until finally the home of the sick man is reached, the god is deposited, and the bearers adjourn.

The visiting god is then importuned by the sorrowing relatives to cure the invalid or, at least, to give them some advice on the subject. Once more the bearers are summoned and the god is taken to an apothecary shop where its advice on the proper drugs to use is asked. To help him out the family points to various articles around the room. If the god remains immobile when they point to a certain drug, the drug is useless, but if he moves (due to accidental moving by the bearers) the family purchases the chemical which happens to be in that general direction.

When it becomes certain that the sick man is going to die in spite of all precautions (or perhaps because of them) the family set about getting his dying outfit together. If the sufferer is a man he must be provided with boots and a ceremonial head-dress. The soles of the boots are soft and flexible so that they will not hurt his feet on his journey to Heaven. Next comes a long gown and an overcoat. Neither garment must have brass buttons, of which the Chinese are usually very fond. Brass buttons, however, would weigh down the deceased so that he could not ascend to Heaven so easily. The underwear must be padded, even in the hottest weather, as must the trousers and waistcoats. The Chinese believe that padded clothing keeps the corpse from putrefaction. Women are clothed in a long gown, an over-mantle, a veil, and padded under-clothing.

All of the clothing, of course, is new. None of it must be fur lined or otherwise contaminated by animal skins for there is a superstition that should the deceased come into contact with anything from an animal the departed soul returns to earth as an animal.

Significance of Colours. — All colours may be used but red and yellow are reserved for scholars and officials. White is only used by the very poor people as colour costs money in China. Silk and satin are used if possible. Fastenings of all sorts are left off the garments and a simple string is tied around the waist. The usual girdle is believed to be used to carry off children and it is thought that should a girdle be included in the dead man's wardrobe he might be lonesome and take a child with him.

A dying man is not permitted to lie in a family bed for, in that case, the bed would be forever haunted. Usually a door is laid across two trestles and the dying man is placed on it, even though moving him may hasten death.

No curtains are allowed in the room where a dying man lies, because curtains are thought to resemble fish-nets and the mourners fear that he might turn into a fish if his last hours were so influenced. Pillows are removed, for should the dying man happen to gaze upon his feet, if only to look at his new boots, misfortune would then befall the children. By lowering the head this dire possibility is eliminated.

ANCESTOR WORSHIP

In the majority of homes in China, no matter how great or how humble, there is a domestic shrine or temple before which members of the family worship daily. In April of every year people gather at family graves to worship the departed.

Many children necessarily worship at the graves of ancestors whom they have never seen, but as they grow older those ancestors are exchanged for nearer ones, grandmothers and grandfathers who held them when they were babies or first taught them to walk.

Ancestor worship extends back only to immediate ancestors.

All this tends to make family relations stronger and to build a lasting tie between brothers and sisters. It produces the filial obedience and reverence for which China has long been famed. Although ancestor worship arises from purely superstitious motives it inevitably makes for the tremendous strength of the Chinese people as a race, their close affiliations and habits of clinging together in every walk of life.

Bird Parade. — As is well-known, the Chinese are great lovers of cage birds, and an unusual proof of this can be witnessed early morning or late afternoon of any fine day on the South section of Thibet Road, opposite the Race Course. Here scores of fanciers adjourn, for the purpose of displaying and "airing" their pets, which are of many types and sizes. The commercial side is not altogether lost sight of and the owner of some particular songster may occasionally be induced to part with it for a consideration.

Chapter Fourteen
ARTS AND CRAFTS

TEA INDUSTRY

CHINA'S great tea industry dates back a thousand years to the T'ang Dynasty (about the beginning of the ninth century) when "learned men and poets" first introduced tea as a beverage. Since then it has become the favourite liquid refreshment of the countless millions of the Far East and possesses ceremonial significance as its service to a guest is regarded as a token of respect and hospitality.

Tea in China is cultivated principally in the eight provinces of Kiangsu, Chekiang, Anhwei, Fukien, Kiangsi, Hunan, Hupeh and Yunnan. High grade tea is produced in mountainous regions and a moist atmosphere is desirable.

Tea is classified into three groups, Black, Green, and Flower (or Scented Tea). Orange Pekoe, Oolong and Suchong are among the Black Teas. There are more varieties of green tea, and among these, consumed by most Chinese, are Hangchow Green Tea (Flat Hyson), Yellow Mountain Tea, etc. These are high grade green teas and are uncolored. Green teas are sometimes printed and dyed.

Due to its fragrance and delightful taste, the consumption of Flower Tea increases yearly. The method of curing is to bake green or black tea with fresh flowers. Jasmine, Rose, Lemon, and Chloranthus are all high grade flower teas.

Owing to its natural fertilization and favourable climatic conditions the quality of Chinese tea is superior. The fragrance of black tea, the delightful taste of green tea, and delicious flavor of flower tea are beyond comparison.

Many visitors to Shanghai take advantage of the opportunity to purchase a specially packed chest of tea to take home. Excellent service of this nature is given by the Wang Yue Tai Tea Co.

SILK

One of the most important industries of China is the growing and weaving of silk. About two-thirds of the silk produced in China is consumed within the country, the balance being exported.

Chinese history credits the invention of silk to Yuen Fei, the concubine of an Emperor who ruled in 2,600 B.C. She, by reason of the discovery, has been deified and is worshipped as the goddess of silk worms. For many centuries after Yuen Fei the secret of silk was jealously guarded by the Chinese.

The chief food of the silk worms is the leaf of the mulberry tree, which is cultivated carefully in China. The trees live about 50 years. The cultivated trees are about six feet tall while the wild mulberry is about 40 feet high. The finest silk is produced from worms fed on leaves of the smaller, domestic tree while the coarser silks, including pongee, are produced from worms which feed on oak leaves. When there are plenty of mulberry leaves the eggs of the worms are hatched artificially, either in incubator trays or, more commonly, by the peasants themselves who carry the eggs next to their bodies to keep them warm or put them between blankets beneath their beds.

One ounce of eggs produces about 20,000 worms, and these worms during their lifetime consume a ton of mulberry leaves. They increase their weight 10,000 times from the day they are hatched to the time when they begin to spin their cocoons. They are carefully tended. The peasants believe that noise is very harmful for the worms and are careful not to startle them. Should visitors go to a plantation they should not be surprised if the caretaker goes ahead of them to inform the worms, so that they will not be frightened. From the time they are hatched the worms are fed with plenty of leaves. At maturity they are about two inches long.

Cocoons are spun from the tops of loose stalks of straw and two or three days only are needed to complete the spinning. Then the cocoons are gathered and the chrysalis killed by heat-ing and drying the cocoons or by packing them with leaves and salt in a jar which is buried in the ground. Were this not done the moth would break through the sheath. In spite of the prevalence of modern machinery and methods, a great quantity of beautiful silk is still produced by the old-fashioned hand reels and looms. The cycle of the ordinary silk worm extends over the year, but some produce two to seven crops annually

PORCELAIN

Undoubtedly the most beautiful and valuable porcelain in the world has been made in China. During the Chou dynasty (1122 to 249 B.C.) the potter's wheel became known and is told of in books of that period, describing the differences of pottery moulded by hand and that made on the wheel. Glaze was discovered during the earlier Han dynasty (206 B.C. to A.D. 25). At that time the glaze was of a dark green colour and so hard that it could not be scratched with a knife.

The industry began to flourish during the T'ang dynasty in the seventh century, when it was established under royal patronage and an Imperial factory was established. The porcelain of that era has been described in annals of the time as "blue as the sky, fragile as paper, bright as a mirror, and sonorous as a plaque of jade stone."

The effect known as "crackle" was discovered in the eighth century by accident and developed to a high state of perfection by the Chinese. The porcelain, while being fired, is exposed to a sudden drop of temperature, which causes the glaze to contract more rapidly than the body and break into crackles. The Chinese potters have perfected the process to such an extent that they can now produce any size of crackle desired.

Ming Porcelain.—It was probably during the Ming dynasty (1368 to 1644 A.D.) that the most glorious porcelain was produced, for at about this time the Chinese came into contact with Persian coloured wares and began imitating them, hence the gorgeous cobalt blue and copper tones, the only Persian paints able to stand up under the fierce heat of Chinese kilns. Green porcelain, imitation of jade, was also achieved during this time. Another ware of this period was the eggshell porcelain, upon which the delicate and elaborate designs were engraved before firing. Flower designs came in, and the famous "blue and white" sets which are still the favourite among the Chinese.

"Hawthorne" ginger jars belong to the Manchu dynasty (1644 to 1723 A.D.). During the preceding dynasty the Imperial pottery works had often been destroyed during rebellions but they were erected again under the Manchus. The Ch'en Lung reign (1736 to 1796) was distinguished by the highest technical skill and perfection of details and finesse in porcelain. The beautiful "famille rose" reached its highest stage of development and the pink, ruby and rose eggshell plates and dessert services which are so popular were produced during this period.

The modern period of porcelain-making has been distinguished by no remarkable developments. Potters have been imitating Wedgewood and Sevres and making pottery in semi-European style. Only experts are able to determine porcelain by periods as there is much excellent copying done by the modern potters, even the dates and seals being copied to perfection.

North Gate, Chinese City

Cloisonné. — Peiping is the centre of manufacture of this beautiful ware. In its manufacture the design is outlined on a copper base with thin flat wires, usually of copper but sometimes of gold or silver. The wires are soldered on and the cells filled with coloured enamel paste. The piece is fired, the cells again filled, fired again, filled again, and so on until finished. Then a pumice stone is used to grind the enamel to a smooth surface, after which the article is polished.

In the factories at Peiping any design will be copied that is desired and the process may be watched by visitors.

LACQUER

The sap of the lac tree of China is responsible for some of the most beautiful and fascinating wares of the Orient. Centuries ago the Chinese began making pieces of lacquer which have never been excelled any place in the world and to-day the modern but very beautiful red, gold, and black lacquer boxes, trays, coffee sets, finger bowls, etc., which are made in Foochow, are always in demand and may be had at absurdly cheap prices. Much imitation lacquer is also on display in Shanghai.

Authentic lacquer work is made of carefully polished wood covered with layers of silk. Over this a coating of lac, sap drawn from the tree, is spread and covered with a mixture of emery powder, red sandstone and vermillion (or other colours).

After drying the process is repeated about eighteen times. If the piece is to be figured the designs are drawn on heavy paper, marked with pin pricks, transferred to the article by powdered chalk and drawn with a needle. The process is tedious and requires much time. Inferior lacquer is usually the result of insufficient time. The work must be done in dustproof rooms and a certain amount of bravery is connected with every piece inasmuch as the raw lac is extremely irritating to the skin and produces innumerable small boils.

JEWELLERY

Jade, so far as the Chinese are concerned, is the most precious of stones, and any jewellery characteristic of China will, necessarily, contain jade. Some of it, of a clear, apple green colour, is as expensive as diamonds of the same weight. Most foreign buyers, however, are satisfied with other shades at more moderate prices. Many artificial stones from Siberia and Germany are sold as genuine jade while other ornaments offered as jade are nothing but soapstone of a greenish-white colour. This, however, may be easily detected by scratching the article with a knife. If it is real jade it will not scratch and if it is not real jade the dealer will protest vigorously against having it scratched.

Lovely filagree work in gold and silver is produced by Chinese jewellers, and only in China can the beautiful kingfisher feather work jewellery be made.

So many imitations of precious gems are made and sold in China that it is extremely difficult to know what is genuine and what is not.

BRONZE

The oldest form of art in China is bronze work, dating back at least 3,000 years. Important collections existing to-day contain specimens of the Shang and Chou dynasties (1766 to 249 B.C.). These specimens display savage designs in striking contrast to the refined delicacy of other manifestations of Chinese art. Animals, either real or fabulous, were used as decorations.

Genuine early pieces are covered with red, green and brown earthenware, but artificial coloured earthenware is often put on with wax and pass as curios. This deception may be discovered by scraping the bronze with a knife, or by dipping it in boiling water. The genuine earthenware is almost as hard as the bronze itself.

The highest development of bronze work was reached about 500 B.C. The bronze then was magnificently decorated with gold and silver. Early crudities of design and workmanship disappeared and a refinement of form became apparent. The art of bronze work suffered a decline in the Tang dynasty, but was revived in the Sung and Ming dynasties.

PAINTING

Chinese painting more or less has gone hand in hand with the development and decline of porcelain making. It is entirely different from any European standards and needs an adapted point of view for any appreciation whatsoever. Technical details, as in Chinese drama, have little or nothing to do with art, and the more bizarre and fantastic the imagination displayed in dealing with any subject the more truly artistic it is considered.

The very new artists have gone in for modernism in a big way but achieve their effects mainly through imitation of Occidental twentieth century schools.

Early artists spurned realism and confined themselves mainly to lyrical and highly imaginative landscapes and symbolic figures of Chinese religion and history. Perspective in early Chinese art is conspicuous by its absence. In the Chinese mind space and distance cannot possibly exist on the flat surface of a piece of paper or silk.

Some of the old Chinese paintings are very valuable, the value usually not being determined by quality but by association. The old custom of inscribing poems and epigrams on the margins of pictures has left a remarkable collection of paintings with comments or verse by numerous famous men throughout the centuries. The result is of far more historical importance and interest than artistic.

All Chinese paintings are on silk or paper scrolls, which are rolled up and unfolded when hung. Many of the older paintings have been stored away in rolls for hundreds of years, in dark cabinets, hence the illusion of fresh colouring which so often prevails in an old Chinese painting.

*   *   *

The Chinese credit Ts'ai Lun, A.D. 105, with the invention of paper.

Chapter Fifteen
MISCELLANEA

SETTLEMENT ROADS. — The length of the roads under the control of the Shanghai Municipal Council is a fraction more than 182 miles.

* * *

Salaries of Officials. — Executive officials of the International Settlement (S.M.C.) are paid on a standard comparable with other great cities. Annual salaries: Secretary General, $41,960; Commissioner of Police, $38,600; Commissioner of Public Works, $38,600; Treasurer and Controller, $38,600; Commissioner of Public Health, $29,380; Commandant of Shanghai Volunteer Corps, $28,110; Chief Officer of Fire Brigade, $21,820; Conductor of Municipal Orchestra and Band, $16,360.

* * *

Cost of Government. — The Shanghai Municipal Council (the

Lunghua Pagoda

[206]

following statistics pertain only to the International Settlement) according to the budget for 1934 will have a total income of almost exactly $49,000,000, balanced by estimated expenditures. Income and expenses are both listed under two headings, ordinary and extraordinary, almost evenly divided.

Ordinary revenue, which provides for general administrative expenses of the International Settlement, is derived from license fees and other sundry sources but principally from a land tax of seven-tenths of one per cent., payable by renters of property assessed at $1,057,670,749, less $70,158,321, the value of municipal and exempted properties; a general municipal tax rate of 14 per cent. on the assessed rentals of buildings, foreign houses within the Settlement being assessed at $47,000,000 and Chinese houses at $37,000,000, and a special rate of 12 per cent. on assessed rentals of buildings beyond the International Settlement limits (in the extra-Settlement Roads areas), the assessment on foreign houses in these districts being $6,404,000 and Chinese, $400,000.

Extraordinary income is derived from a sinking fund, sale of surplus land, and from the issuance of debentures or other temporary measures. Extraordinary expenditures are for construction and maintenance of public buildings and works, purchase of new equipment, in short for capital investments rather than for operating expenses.

Parks. — Parks in Shanghai are well kept and verdantly lovely. In the International Settlement are Jessfield Park, Hongkew Park, and the Public Garden. There is the Koukaza Garden in the French Concession. Jessfield Park is the largest and most beautiful, with splendid flower beds, hothouses, the Municipal Conservatory, ancient trees, and a well stocked zoo. It may be reached by continuing along Bubbling Well Road to the Avenue Haig and Jessfield Road intersection. Either continue along Jessfield Road to St. John's University and enter by way of the zoo, or branch off at the Yu Yuen Road intersection with Jessfield Road and continue to Brennan Road. Jessfield Park is at the intersection of Yu Yuen Road and Brenan Road.

Hongkew Park may be reached by continuing along North Szechuen Road to the Thomas Hanbury School and then turning into Paoshan Road for a distance of a few hundred yards. The park is directly in front of the Municipal Rifle Range used by the Shanghai Volunteer Corps. In this park are a golf course, tennis courts, and a swimming pool.

The Public Garden is directly adjacent to The Bund, just South of the Garden Bridge. The horticulture of this Garden is its chief charm.

The Koukaza Garden is on Rue Lafayette, at the Avenue Dubail intersection. It may also be entered from Route Voyron off Avenue Joffre. It contains a children's playground and has well laid out flower beds.

Twenty cents admission is charged to all of the parks. Season tickets may be purchased for $1.00.

*   *   *

Fireman, Save My Child! — The public Ambulance Service in the International Settlement of Shanghai is operated — and efficiently operated — by the Shanghai Fire Brigade. The Settlement's fire fighting machinery is motorized and is the last word in modernity, in both equipment and organization.

*   *   *

Public Library. — The Shanghai Municipal Council maintains a Public Library at 22 Nanking Road (upstairs).

*   *   *

Swimming Baths. — Those visitors making use of the

Y.M.C.A., the Columbia Country Club, the Cercle Sportif Francais, the Country Club, the Shanghai Rowing Club or the Swimming Bath Club will have the use in each of these institutions of an admirable swimming bath. There is also a public swimming bath adjoining Hongkew Park.

* * *

Houseboating. — Week-end excursions on houseboats are a favourite diversion of Shanghailanders and may be enjoyed by visitors as houseboats, both foreign and Chinese, are available for rental. Houseboating, if time affords, is an excellent way of seeing Chinese rural life and scenery at first hand. Because of the many rivers and canals which make a checkerboard of the vast Yangtsze delta, houseboat trips of amazing distances may be made. To obtain a houseboat, fully equipped and manned, advertise in the local newspapers.

Good Hunting. — There is plenty of wild game in China and excellent hunting may be had in various districts, the game ranging from snipe to tigers and panthers. Game birds, snipe, duck and pheasant, abound in regions contiguous to Shanghai. Deer may be hunted along the Yangtsze. Wild pigs offer good sport in Chekiang Province. Hunters are required to register at their Consulates. Local sporting goods houses will be glad to advise as to official requirements, equipment, and hunting districts.

* * *

Shanghai Goes Motoring. — The number of motor vehicles in Shanghai has increased by 42 per cent. in five years.

* * *

More Passengers. — The Tramway Company transported 119,669,536 passengers in 1933 as against 108,845,656 in 1932.

* * *

Police Marksmanship. — Shanghai policemen are trained in marksmanship. In 32 encounters with armed criminals in 1933 the Police casualties were one killed and eight wounded. Eleven criminals were shot dead and 13 were wounded. Chicago papers please copy.

* * *

Shopping Around.—Peking Road, in the blocks to the West from The Bund, offers much of interest to the tourist. Here are centred secondhand shops, scores of them, dealing in every conceivable variety of merchandise. Some of them take on the aspect of a small museum. Occasionally rare bargains may be obtained. But—one must be a keen bargainer. Don't pay the first price asked; perhaps the third or fourth quotation will be about right. Even then you may be "taken."

* * *

Guilds.—Guilds are to be found in every part of China, some of them dating back for thousands of years. They are divided primarily into three classes, the trade unions, clubs of fellow provincials in an alien city, and associations of merchants for the regulation of trade: the last is more rarely found than the others, while the trade guilds predate the rest by hundreds of years. All craftsmen become members of the guild of their craft: in certain cities the craft is in the hands of aliens who are not allowed to divulge its secrets to the natives. The administration is carried out by a manager, a committee, and a paid secretary who arranges all legal defence, apportions grants for charity, and approaches officials. The revenue is obtained by means of a regular subscription according to the financial standing of the person, and taxes and fines of the members. In addition members may be called upon for extraordinary subscriptions for funeral or doctors' expenses. Members who are caught stealing or in any shady practices are fined heavily and may be expelled or even in severe cases executed. The basic idea of Chinese guilds is to promote general wellbeing among the members and to protect them as far as possible in everything. The four most famous guilds are the Canton Guild, the Shansi Guild, the Shantung Guild, and the Ningpo Guild.

*   *   *

Naval Maneuvers. — During the Summer months the United States Asiatic Fleet, based at the Cavite Navyyard, Philippine Islands, holds maneuvers at Chefoo and Tsingtao, popular Summer resorts North of Shanghai, Tsingtao being situated on the South shore of the Shantung Peninsula and Chefoo on the North. Weihaiwei, near Chefoo on the North shore of the peninsula, is a Summer rendezvous for British warships. Tsingtao and Chefoo are easily accessible from Shanghai by coastwise steamers. They offer much in the way of Summer recreation. Tsingtao is 400 miles from Shanghai, Chefoo 520.

*   *   *

Chinese Become Residents. — The first official proclamation permitting Chinese to reside in the Foreign Settlement, and requiring them to conform to the Land Regulations and contribute to any general assessments, was issued by the Taotai (chief Chinese official in the district) on February 24, 1855.

"Keep to the Left." — The "keep to the left" rule in driving is universal in Shanghai, and, indeed, throughout China and the rest of the Orient, save only in Tsingtao, a Summer resort city in Shantung Province. There the American "keep to the right" rule prevails, due to the fact that Tsingtao is a former German possession; the Germans also "keep to the right." There is a movement, however, to have Tsingtao change to the left-drive rule.

*   *   *

Native Products Movement. — China exports tea, silk, wood oil, soya beans and a few other well known products. Yet there are many other Chinese products which have never been known abroad but which will find a ready market once introduced.

Fostering the rapidly growing movement to popularize native products, not only in foreign markets but within China as well, a group of Shanghai manufacturers and bankers organized the China Native Products Co. (Shanghai), Ltd., on Nanking Road.

It is essentially a department store, selling Chinese products of all descriptions. A visit is worth while as showing China's progress as a producing country. There is beautiful embroidery work made by Hunan girls, porcelain ware from the famous Chin-Teh-Chen where China wares used by royal families of ancient dynasties were made, exquisite stone articles from Wenchow, ivory novelties carved by Cantonese artists, and so on through an endless list to the modern machine-made articles of every description.

The collection suggests an amalgamation of ancient and modern China, of arts and science, of culture and industry.

Encouraged by the initial success, similar organizations are springing up in great cities all over the country. They have now, or soon will have, one each in the following cities: Chenchow,

Nanking, Changsha, Hankow, Canton and Chungking.

Taipings Come Close. — In their second attack on the Foreign Settlement, in January, 1862, the Taiping Rebels, approaching from the direction of Woosung, reached a point one and a half miles from the British Consulate (present location on The Bund). The third attack, in August, 1862, carried the Taipings to the Bubbling Well.

*　　*　　*

Lace and Embroidery. — With the advent of the missionaries, lace-making was introduced to China and has since become a small but important industry. Since in China there are missionaries from every part of the world, every variety and design of lace may be found.

Unlike lace-making the art of embroidery is centuries old and is entirely native to China. Embroidery in China has an older history than in any other country, no doubt because of the first development of the silk industry here. Richest examples of embroidery are to be found on the old Chinese theatrical costumes. One costume, for one actor, has often required the skilled labour of a dozen women for half a dozen years.

*　　*　　*

Tea Was a Vegetable. — The universal beverage of the Chinese is tea. Its earliest use was as a vegetable rather than a drink. The Emperor Wen-ti (589-605 A.D.) was advised by a Buddhist priest to drink boiled tea plant leaves as a remedy for headache. In the eighth century there is evidence of tea growing having become a regular industry, for in the annals of the T'ang Dynasty one learns of its being subjected to an imperial duty.

*   *   *

Elderly Cupid.—Instead of the chubby infant, with his bow and arrows, familiar to Occidentals, an old man is the Cupid of Chinese mythology. He is usually known as "Yueh Hsia Lau Jen," or "Old Man Under the Moon." The romantic influence of the moon has long been established, both East and West.

Highest Pagoda.—Of the some 2,000 pagodas in China, the highest is said to be at Tingchou, Chihli Province, approximately 360 feet.

"Pailous."—These gates or archways are common all over China, serving as memorials. "P'ai" meals tablet and "lou" storey. Early in the Chou Dynasty (B.C. 1122-249) worthy men were honoured by a tablet of distinction being affixed to the gateway of their village. (*see Encyclopaedia Sinica*). Later the practice was adopted of erecting special gateways, or Pailous, to bear the honorific tablets. The commonest type have four pillars, forming a large central passage, flanked by two smaller ones.

These memorial arches were granted to loyal servants of the state who died in war, officials of good reputation, men distinguished by virtue and learning, philanthropists, families that had lived together for four or five generations, centenarians, highest literary graduates, women who were killed or committed suicide in defence of their virtue, and widows who escaped compulsion to re-marry by destroying themselves.

There is a widow's arch on the Race Course and Public Recreation Ground in Shanghai.

*   *   *

"Losing Face."—When Chinese are accused of a fault, publicly reprimanded, apprehended in misbehaviour or theft, or fail to discharge an obligation, they are said to "lose face." The closest English conception of the term "face" is conveyed by "pride." To "lose face" is to suffer a grievous wound of the pride.

The Chinese will do anything to "save face" at whatever cost and trouble, even though it means dismissal from service. The best way to get along with Chinese servants is not to do anything to make them "lose face." If necessary, simply dismiss them and do not discuss the matter.

The first public meeting held in Shanghai took place at the British Consulate on April 12, 1844. Sir George Balfour, British Consul, acted as chairman of the gathering, which met to consider the purchase of a burial ground "to the west of the ditch at the back of the Custom House."

Chapter Sixteen
HISTORICAL ODDMENTS

"WHEN Shih Hwang-ti, who built the Great Wall of China (the work was started about 215 B.C. and required only ten years for completion) captured the (Yangtsze) delta, he made Shanghai a hsien district and during the Sung Dynasty (960-1127 A.D.) the name of Shanghai began to be used, the first mention being chronicled in 1075 A.D. Before the foreigners came and made it China's largest port, it was only a small fishing port enclosed by a wall (the Chinese City) to protect it against the inroads of Japanese pirates, and could boast of no more importance than being a port of call for seagoing junks and the home of a fishing fleet of about 400 junks."

— Crow's *Handbook for China.*

* * *

Shih Hwang-ti Duke of Tsin, who built the Great Wall as a protection against Tartars after trying for ten years to overcome them (*see* Couling's *Encyclopaedia Sinica,* page 218), has been referred to as a saviour of China, the only man strong enough to unite the country, which had been rent by continual internal warfare, under one rule. He is said to have established the Ch'in Dynasty (249-206 B.C.) from which the modern name China was derived.

* * *

"Shanghai lies in the south-east corner of that portion of the Province of Kiangsu to the South of the Yangtsze. Kiangsu and portions of the neighbouring provinces of Chekiang and Anhuei form a vast plain, owing its origin to the fine silt brought down in the course of ages by the Yangtsze and deposited in the sea. The physical features of the district have, therefore, undergone enormous changes since the day when Wuhu was the head of the delta of the Yangtsze-kiang, and that river found its way to the sea by three mouths at least. Even in historic times these changes have been great. In A.D. 780 the Soochow Creek is said to have been five miles broad, and the Soochow Creek was the main stream, the Whangpoo flowing only as far as Loonghwa (Lunghua), finding its way to the sea by another channel. These changes still continue: the Whangpoo is said to be at least two hundred yards narrower than it was thirty years ago, and the Soochow Creek, in the mouth of which the British fleet anchored in 1843, now affords a passage for boats only in mid-channel."

Shanghai, a Handbook for Travellers and Residents, by the Rev. C. E. Darwent, M.A., former Minister of Union Church.

*   *   *

"In A.D. 446 the Viceroy of Yangchow, in whose jurisdiction the place lay, was ordered by Imperial rescript to cut a canal to link up the city of Soochow with the Yangtsze. This being done seems to have marked the beginning of Shanghai's importance as an anchorage. Its sheltered position, its proximity to the important centres of Soochow, Sungkiang and Hangchow together with the gradual silting up of the nearer approaches to the first two of the above-named places, all helped little by little to make

Mandarin Garden, Chinese City

the port a favourite rendezvous for deep-water junks and a point for the trans-shipment of their cargoes.

"In the last years of the thirteenth century, either in 1288 or in 1292 (in which latter year, it is interesting to remember, the great Venetian traveller, Marco Polo, finally quitted China) the original town together with several adjacent villages was erected by an ordinance of the great Kublai Khan, the Mongol conqueror, then Emperor of China, into a 'hsien' or city of sub-prefectural status.

"From about this time the growing wealth of the place seems to have attracted the unwelcome attentions of Japanese pirates, and the records speak frequently of raids. It would also appear that the Japanese were not the only offenders, since later references to 'black slaves' and 'white devils' indicate that Malayan and Portuguese freebooters may have occasionally preyed upon the trade of the port. The Japanese adventurers established a pirates nest on Tsungming Island, lying in the Yangtsze directly opposite the mouth of the Whangpoo, from whence they levied a heavy tribute upon all corners.

"The most serious pirate raid occurred in 1554, when the city was looted and burned, and in the following year the citizens for their protection surrounded themselves with a substantial wall, three miles in circumference (the present Chinese City)."

— Gow's *Guide to Shanghai (1924)*

*   *   *

"History is not quite clear when Shanghai first came into being; a writer in the 'North China Daily News' some years ago says it was known to exist B.C. 304. Lanning in his *History of Shanghai* says that it was not until A.D. 960 that the name, Shanghai, had established itself . . . . . .

"At any rate it is proved that the site whereon the city is, was once sea and that the country for hundreds of miles around has been formed by the silt brought down by the Yangtsze river, and the fine alluvial soil thus deposited being exceptionally rich, was most suitable for settlers, the country soon developing into a prosperous agricultural and fishing district.

"The earliest site in Shanghai history is the temple at the end of Bubbling Well Road, known as Ching An Ssu, which, it is claimed, dates back to 250 A.D. and owes its popularity to the famous well opposite with its mixture of carbonic acid and marsh gas." (*See* "Nanking and Bubbling Well Roads" in Chapter Six, "Seeing Shanghai," in *All About Shanghai and Environs*).

The three quoted paragraphs are from *Guide to Shanghai* by A. G. Hickmott (1921).

*   *   *

"Handed down by legends, Chinese history begins about 2,500 B.C. with the reign of the three emperors, who in a remarkably short space of time brought a barbarous people to a comparatively high stage of civilization. The first of these semi-mythical rulers was Fu Hsi (or Fuhi), who instituted marriage, taught the people to fish with nets, domesticated the wild animals for their use, invented the flute and lyre and replaced former methods of communication (by means of knots tied in strings) with a kind of picture language which has been succeeded by the present Chinese ideographs.

"His grave is now pointed out in Chechow, Henan, where thousands assemble annually to do reverence to his memory.

"The following emperor, Shen Nung, carried the advance of the people still further. He taught agriculture and the use of herbs as medicine, and is now known as 'The Imperial Husbandman.' The third emperor, Hwang-ti, extended the boundaries of the empire, reformed the calendar, established cities, and introduced the use of carts and boats, while his consort taught the rearing of silkworms. Foreign historians regard these three emperors as merely representative of different stages of early civilization, while the Chinese ascribe to them supernatural qualities."

– Crow's *Handbook for China.*

Chapter Seventeen
LEAVING SHANGHAI

WHERE next? To the traveller, Shanghai offers a unique advantage; the entire world, literally, is open for his selection. He can go to Europe by going West, or he can go to Europe by going East, with distances, time, and cost showing but slight variation. It may be an exaggeration to call Shanghai the "centre of the world" but it looks very much like it on a travel map.

Most Occidentals will recall a youthful legend: "Dig a hole through the earth and you will come out in China." With equal aptness it may be said, "Start out from China and go anywhere you like, in almost any direction." Transportation facilities to any other place in the world are readily available in Shanghai.

Go East or West. — A trip to Europe may be made to the West by sea through the Suez Canal or by train through Siberia and Russia; to the East by sea across the Pacific Ocean, overland across the United States or Canada and across the Atlantic, or entirely by sea through the Panama Canal. One can go to London by travelling either West or East; one can go to New York by travelling either East or West.

Perhaps the world is round after all.

Travelling by sea to the East, Japan and the Hawaiian Islands are on the schedules of most of the liners bound for the Pacific coast of the United States and Canada while ships for Europe going West via the Suez Canal usually call (with some exceptions) at Hongkong, Manila, Saigon, Singapore, Malacca, Penang, Colombo, Aden, Port Said, Naples, Marseilles, Gibraltar, and London. All travel agencies and steamship offices can give detailed advices as to ports of call offered by different services.

Steamship Services to Europe. — Herewith are listed some of the services available from Shanghai:

Blue Funnel Line (Butterfield and Swire): Shanghai to Lon-

don, five weeks; three sailings per month via Hongkong, Singapore, Penang, Colombo, Port Said; first class £88, second class £68-64.

Hamburg-Amerika Line, 20 Canton Road: Shanghai to Hamburg, 35 days by boat to Genoa, 30 hours by train to Hamburg; monthly service via Hongkong, Manila, Straits, Colombo, Port Said, Genoa, Marseilles, Barcelona, Rotterdam, Hamburg; cabin class £74.

Java-China-Japan Lijn, 133 Szechuen Road: main service to Dutch East Indies via Manila, and connecting services with Dutch Mails to Europe, South Africa and Australia.

Lloyd Triestino, 170 Kiangse Road (Hamilton House): Shanghai to Venice, twenty-four days; monthly service via Hongkong, Singapore, Colombo, Bombay, Port Said and Brindisi; first class to Venice £98; second class £68.

Messageries Maritimes (French Mail), 9-10 French Bund: Shanghai to Marseilles, thirty or thirty-two days; fortnightly service via Hongkong, Saigon, Singapore, Colombo, Djibouti, Port Said; first class A grade £98, B grade £94; second class £65.

Nippon Yusen Kaisha (Japanese Mail), 31 The Build: Shanghai to London, five weeks; fortnightly service via Hongkong, Singapore, Malacca, Penang, Aden, Port Said, Naples, Marseilles, Gibraltar; first class £99, second class £66.

Norddeutscher Lloyd, 210 Kiukiang Road: Shanghai to Hamburg, forty-six days; monthly service via Hongkong, Manila, Singapore, Belawan, Colombo, Port Said, Genoa, Barcelona, Lisbon, Dover, Rotterdam; first class £77, inter-

Sampan

mediate class £44.

Peninsular & Oriental Steam Navigation Co. (P. and O.), 17 Canton Road (Mackinnon, Mackenzie & Co.): Shanghai to Marseilles, thirty days; special P. & O. express from Marseilles to London, twenty-three hours; fortnightly service via Hongkong, Singapore, Penang, Colombo, Bombay, Aden, Port Said, Malta, Marseilles, Gibraltar, Tangier; first class to London, £98, second class £68.

Dollar Steamship Line, 51 Canton Road: Around the world service, West-bound; Shanghai to New York, fifty-six days; fortnightly service via Manila, Singapore, Penang, Colombo, Bombay, Port Said, Alexandria, Naples, Genoa, Marseilles; first class £127, tourist class £82. (From New York one may complete the trip around the world back to Shanghai by way of Havana, the Panama Canal, Los Angeles, San Francisco, Honolulu, and Japan).

To Europe Overland.—In going to Europe via Siberia one may travel by steamship to Dairen, where train connections are made for Moscow. The sea voyage requires two days and the ships call at Tsingtao. First class fare to Dairen is $90, second class $60.

Going to Europe direct by rail one must go first to Harbin, fare $144 (Mex.) from Shanghai. From Harbin to Moscow fare is U.S. $146. Twelve days are required for the trip from Shanghai to Moscow. From Moscow to Berlin will cost U.S. $22, two days; from Berlin to Paris is a day and costs U.S. $10.

To U.S.A. and Canada.—Trans-Pacific services from Shanghai to the United States and Canada, whence transcontinental rail and trans-Atlantic connections to Europe may be made, are available as follows:

American Mail Line (Dollar), 51 Canton Road: fortnightly direct to Victoria (Vancouver) and Seattle via Japan, fourteen days; first class U.S. $331, second class U.S. $185.

Canadian Pacific, 4 The Bund: Shanghai to America and Canada, fortnightly service direct to Victoria and Vancouver, via Japan, 15 days; fortnightly service to Victoria and Vancouver, via Honolulu, 18 days; first class U.S. $331-356, tourist class U.S. $185-215.

Dollar Line, 51 Canton Road: Shanghai to San Francisco, fortnightly service to San Francisco via Japan and Honolulu, 15 to 17 days; first class U.S. $346-356, special class U.S. $185-215.

Nippon Yusen Kaisha, 31 The Bund: Shanghai to San Francisco via Japan and Honolulu, eighteen days; first class U.S. $356, second class U.S. $215; Shanghai to Los Angeles, 21 days; first class U.S. $356, second class U.S. $220; Shanghai to Seattle direct, via Japan, 12 days from Yokohama (fare from Shanghai to Yokohama, and hotel expenses paid by steamship company), first class U.S. $290, second class U.S. $150.

States Steamship Co., 170 Kiangse Road, Hamilton House: service every three weeks to Pacific Coast ports via Japan, direct from Yokohama; 19 days to San Francisco, U.S. $198; 21 days to Portland, U.S. $208; one class only.

Australia and New Zealand. — Japan and Shanghai passengers for Australian-Oriental Line travel by Canadian Pacific and Dollar Line to Hongkong. Those booked for Eastern and Australian S.S. Co., Ltd., and Nippon Yusen Kaisha can also avail themselves of passage by any line to Hongkong at the steamship company's option. Passengers booked on N.Y.K. line can proceed from Shanghai to Nagasaki to join steamer instead of changing at Hongkong. The three lines each have monthly services to Sydney and Melbourne; fares from Shanghai to Sydney, connecting in Hongkong, £53 first class, £33 second class; from Shanghai via Japan first class £56, second class £35-10; from Shanghai to Melbourne, connecting at Hongkong, £54 first class, £34-5 second class; from Shanghai via Japan, first class £57-5, second class £37-5; 18 days to Australia when connecting at Hongkong, 31 days from Shanghai via Japan. Fares from Australia to New Zealand are £10 first class, £8 second class, two days. Australian-Oriental Line (Butterfield and Swire); Eastern and Australian Steamship Co., 17 Canton Road (Mackinnon, Mackenzie & Co.); Nippon Yusen Kaisha, 31 The Bund.

Coast and River Routes.—Shanghai is the centre of an extremely active coastwise and river trade. Steamers depart almost daily for Canton, Swatow, Wenchow and Amoy, to the South; and for Chefoo, Tsingtao, Tientsin, N'ewchwang and Dairen, to the North.

The mighty Yangtsze provides a splendid waterway into Central China. Hankow is accessible by large steamers at all seasons, while smaller craft proceed many hundreds of miles farther into the interior.

Distances from Shanghai.—By nautical miles from Shanghai to—

North:		South:	
Tsingtao	400	Ningpo	136
Weihaiwei	480	Wenchow	344
Chefoo	520	Foochow	440
Dairen	560	Amoy	600
Newchwang	700	Swatow	730

Tientsin	730		Hongkong	850
			Kwangchowwan	1,083
Korea:			Haiphong	1,335
Chemulpo	503		Saigon	1,780
Gensan	784			
			(East Indian Ports)	
Formosa:			(Via Hongkong):	
Tamsui	453		Manila	1,493
			Manila (direct)	1,162
Japan:			Singapore	2,293
Nagasaki	450		Penang	2,600
Moji-Shimonoseki	550		Batavia	2,825
Kobe	760		Rangoon	3,330
Yokohama	1,100			
Siberia:			India:	
Vladivostok	1,000		Colombo	3,900
			Calcutta	4,067
Arabia:			Madras	4,450
Aden	6,000		Bombay	4,753
			Karachi	5,236
Africa:				
Zanzibar	6,476		Europe:	
Alexandria	7,600		Athens	7,963
Capetown	8,320		Constantinople	8,084
			Brindisi	8,218
Australia & New Zealand:			Odessa	8,248
Brisbane	4,955		Genoa	8,739
Sydney	5,429		Marseilles	8,800
Melbourne	6,005		Barcelona	8,888
Auckland (N.Z.)	6,693		Gibraltar	9,199
			Cherbourg	10,330
Pacific Islands:			Southampton	10,342
Honolulu	4,409		Liverpool	10,504
Suva	5,385		London	10,541

American Ports:

West Coast:

Seattle	5,289
Victoria	5,230
San Francisco	5,491
Los Angeles	5,673
Panama	9,120
Valparaiso	11,149

Antwerp	10,721
Rotterdam	10,746
Hamburg	10,968
Bergen	11,147
Gothenburg	11,120
Copenhagen	11,252
Leningrad	11,823

American Ports:

East Coast	Via Suez	Via Panama
New York	12,405	10,684
Quebec	12,177	11,720
N. Orleans	13,650	9,998

	Via Suez	Via Panama
Havana	13,165	9,699
Trinidad	12,530	9,820
Rio de Janeiro	14,450	13,670

Sunset Over the Whangpoo

APPENDIX ONE

POLICE POWERS

A further definition of the operative organizations for the policing of the International Settlement than is contained in the main body of this book (*see* Chapter Two, "Governments of Shanghai," under sub-heading, "French Procedure") seems advisable on the basis of information received from responsible officials of the Shanghai Municipal Council.

While it is true, broadly speaking, that police authority is vested in the respective organizations of the French Concession and the International Settlement there are other agencies exercising the right of arrest within certain limitations.

The Japanese Government maintains in the International Settlement a considerable staff of Consular Police, at times estimated as high as 250. They do not interfere with the Municipal Police in the general police administration of the Hongkew district, but they do upon occasion arrest their own nationals on warrants issued by the Japanese consular authorities without reference to the Municipal Police.

The Marshal attached to the United States Court for China is empowered to execute warrants of arrest on American citizens issued by the American authorities without reference to the Municipal Police.

To quote our authority: "Under the extraterritorial rights possessed by the Treaty Powers, there appears to be no question of their authority to exercise certain police functions over their own nationals in this Settlement."

The various Powers who have military or naval forces stationed in Shanghai often have military or naval patrols who function in the Settlement and deal with their own enlisted men at times irrespective of the Municipal Police.

APPENDIX TWO

CHRONOLOGY AND HISTORICAL DIGEST OF MODERN SHANGHAI

1832: First attempt, a failure, to open Shanghai to foreign trade, made by Mr. Hugh Hamilton Lindsay, sent from Macao on a commercial mission by the East India Company. Local Chinese authorities ruled foreign trade must still be restricted to Canton.

1842, August 29: Treaty of Nanking signed, terminating "Opium War" between Great Britain and China, which had inception over trade disputes at Canton. Article Two reads: "His Majesty the Emperor of China agrees that British Subjects, with their families and establishments, shall be allowed to reside, for the purpose of carrying on their Mercantile pursuits, without molestation or restraint at the Cities and Towns of Canton, Amoy, Foochow-fu, Ningpo, and Shanghai, and Her Majesty the Queen of Great Britain, etc., will appoint Superintendents or Consular Officers, to reside at each of the above-named Cities or Towns, to be the medium of communication between the Chinese Authorities and the said Merchants, and to see that the just Duties and other Dues of the Chinese Government as hereafter provided for, are duly discharged by Her Britannic Majesty's Subjects."

1843, November 17: Shanghai opened to foreign trade as a Treaty Port, following ratification of the Treaty of Nanking.

1844, July 3: Treaty signed between the United States and China, giving Americans same right as British to trade in Treaty Ports, and containing first explicit definition of extraterritoriality as it applies to China. Article XXI of the Treaty reads:

"Subjects of China who may be guilty of any criminal act towards citizens of the United States shall be arrested and punished by the Chinese authorities according to the laws of China, and citizens of the United States who may commit any crime in China shall be subject to be tried and punished only by the Consul or other public functionary of the United States thereto authorized according to the laws of the United States; and in order to secure the prevention of all controversy and disaffection, justice shall be equitably and impartially administered on both sides."

Extension of extraterritoriality to civil cases was embraced in Article XXV of the same treaty, reading: "All questions in regard to rights, whether of property or person, arising between citizens of the United States in China, shall be subject to the jurisdiction of, and regulated by the authorities of their own Government, and all controversies occurring in China between citizens of the United States and subjects of any other Government shall be regulated by the treaties existing between the United States and such Governments, respectively, without interference on the part of China."

1844, October 24: France signs treaty with China, acquiring same rights to trade in Treaty Ports as those granted to Great Britain and the United States.

1845, November 29: First Land Regulations promulgated, containing partial definition of original area of Foreign Settlement.

1846, September 20: First delimitation of Foreign Settlement boundaries, enclosing area of approximately 138 acres.

1848, November 27: Foreign Settlement extended to Defence Creek, increasing area to 470 acres.

1848: American Episcopal Church Mission, under Bishop William J. Boone, first Anglican Bishop in China, establishes headquarters North of Soochow Creek, in Hongkew village, the beginning of the American Settlement.

1849, April 6: French Concession boundaries defined; area 164 acres.

1851: By proclamation of Chinese authorities merchants of all nations are permitted to build in Foreign Settlement, a privilege theretofore regarded by British as exclusive for their nationals.

1851: Beginning of Taiping Rebellion, plotted in Canton.

1853, April 12: Birthday of Shanghai Volunteer Corps: Consuls of original Treaty Powers, Great Britain, United States, and France, met with foreign residents, decision reached to organize Volunteer Corps for protection of Settlement.

1853, September 7: Rebels, "Small Swords," but not recognized by Taipings, captured Chinese City (old walled city) of Shanghai.

1854, February: United States Consul established Consulate in Hongkew, near Episcopal Mission, raising American flag and advancing general recognition of Settlement.

1854, April 4: Battle of Muddy Flat (on site of present Race Course), in which British and American naval forces, with Shanghai Volunteers, and suddenly and unexpectedly reinforced by "Small Swords" rebels from beleaguered Chinese City, attacked camp of Imperial troops near the then western boundary of the Settlement, to enforce demand of British Consul that troops be removed to safe distance from Settlement. Imperialists gave way. First baptism of fire for Shanghai Volunteers.

1854, July 11: Public meeting of foreign residents adopted new Land Regulations, authorized and chose first elective Municipal Council, which held first meeting.

1854, July 12: Custom House, disorganized by Taiping-Imperial warfare, re-opened under foreign supervision of representatives of Great Britain, United States, and France, acting with concurrence of Chinese authorities; birthday of present Chinese Maritime Customs.

1855, February 17: "Small Swords" evacuate Chinese City, forced out by joint attack of Imperialists and French forces, French being angered by current, apparently true, reports that British and Americans were trading with rebels.

1855, February 24: Proclamation of Taotai (chief Chinese official), stated conditions subject to which Chinese would be permitted to reside in Foreign Settlement.

1860, June: Taipings capture Soochow.

1860, August 17: First Taiping attack on Chinese City and Foreign Settlement.

1861, October 29: French Concession extended by 23 acres.

1862, January: Second Taiping attack on Settlement, from direction of Woosung, reached point one and a half miles from British Consulate.

1862, May 1: Separate Municipal Council established for administration of French Concession.

1862, August: Third Taiping attack on Settlement reached Bubbling Well.

1862, September 21: Frederick Townsend Ward, American organizer and commander of "Ever Victorious Army," fighting Taipings, killed in action near Ningpo.

1863, June 25: U.S. Consul George F. Seward and Chinese authorities delimit boundaries of American Settlement, area 1,309 acres.

1863, September 21: Agreement made to amalgamate Foreign (British) and American settlements.

1863, December: Actual fusion of settlements consummated.

1863, December 4: "Ever Victorious Army," under "Chinese" Gordon, Ward's British successor, wrests Soochow from Taipings.

1864, May 1: Establishment of Mixed Court in Settlement.

1864, July: Nanking retaken by Imperialists and Taiping Rebellion crushed.

1865: Establishment of H.B.M.'s Supreme Court for China.

1866: Formation of Volunteer Fire Brigade in Settlement.

1870: Control of Shanghai Volunteer Force handed over to Municipal Council.

1874: Serious riots in French Concession over decision to construct road through Ningpo Guild cemetery. Volunteer Corps called out.

1880, August 31: Agreement for provision of water supply for Settlement signed.

1889: Erection of first modern cotton mill in Shanghai.

1890: Council took over existing Eurasian School (Thomas Hanbury School) and converted it into first Municipal School for Foreigners.

1893: Purchase of Electric Light company by Municipal Council.

1894-5: War between China and Japan.

1894, January 25: Japan agreed to regard Shanghai as outside the zone of warfare.

1896: Treaty of Shimonoseki between China and Japan.

1896, July 21: Supplementary Treaty of Commerce between China and Japan signed at Peking, giving Japanese right to carry on trade, industries and manufactures at all Treaty Ports.

1897, April 5: Wheelbarrow riots in Shanghai as result of Council's decision to increase wheelbarrow licenses. Volunteers called out.

1897, May 10: First foreign (British) cotton mill opened in Shanghai.

1898: Railway, Shanghai to Woosung, opened.

1898: Municipal Public Health Department organized by Dr. Stanley.

1899, July: Two large additions to International Settlement delimited, in Yangtszepoo district and to the West, totaling 3,804 acres.

1900, January 27: Area of 171 acres added to French Concession.

1900, March 13: Ratepayers' Meeting sanctioned first grant for Chinese education in Settlement, group of Chinese residents contributing funds for building.

1900, June 20: Boxer outbreak. Anti-foreignism had been growing for months but on this date edicts were issued at Peking for the extermination of all foreigners. Agreement was reached between foreign Consuls and Viceroys of Central Provinces under which Viceroys promised to prevent spread of Boxer rebellion in their provinces provided foreign military operations were confined to North. As precautionary measure defence of International Settlement was in hands of Shanghai Volunteers pending arrival of foreign troops.

1900, August 17: Foreign troops garrison Settlement.

1902: Foreign garrison withdrawn.

1905, December 8: Mixed Court riots resulting from agitation over jurisdiction and care of prisoners. Volunteers called out.

1906, June 30: United States Court for China established by Act of Congress.

1907: Chinese Company added to Shanghai Volunteer Corps.

1908: Shanghai-Nanking railway completed.

1910, November 10: Plague riots in Shanghai, resulting from opposition to enforcement of Public Health by-laws for prevention of plague. Volunteers called out.

1911, October 9: Outbreak of Republican Revolution, led by Dr. Sun Yat-sen.

1911, November 3: Chinese City falls into possession of Revolutionists. Volunteers mobilized for possible defence of Settlement.

1911, November 4: Chinese in Shanghai area accept new republican regime by acclamation.

1911, November 11: Mixed Court taken over by Consular Body.

1912, January 1: Establishment of Republic of China.

1913, July 26: Fighting near International Settlement between Peking Government forces and Kiangsu Province rebels. Consular Body issued declaration of neutrality of Settlement, Chapei and Soochow Creek. Volunteers mobilized. Naval forces landed by British, German, Austrian and Italian warships.

1914, April 8: Chinese-French Convention for extension of Concession boundaries and appointment of two Chinese to advise French Municipal Council.

1914, July 20: Extension proclamation adds 2,167 acres to French Concession, constituting more than 80 per cent. of its present area.

1915: Shanghai-Hangchow railway completed.

1917, August 14: China declared war on Germany and Austria-Hungary.

1918, July 16-19: Riots in Hongkew owing to friction between Japanese and Chinese. Volunteers called out.

1919, May 1: Shanghai Fire Brigade, hitherto volunteer organization, re-organized on professional basis.

1919, June: Strikes and anti-Japanese boycott. Volunteers mobilized to protect property of public utility companies and aid police to preserve order.

1920, April 7: Appointment of Chinese Advisory Committee for Shanghai Municipal Council approved by Ratepayers' meeting.

1920, October 14: Formation of Chinese Ratepayers' Association.

1924, August—to end of 1925: Kiangsu-Chekiang provincial war.

1924, September 9: Municipal Council declared State of Emergency and mobilized Volunteer Corps; naval forces landed from British, American, Japanese and Italian warships, forming defence cordon around International Settlement and French Concession.

1925, January: Volunteers mobilized to aid in disarming and interning 10,000 Chinese soldiers, fugitives, who surrendered either to Concession or Settlement authorities.

1925, May 30: Labour troubles starting in February culminated in procession and attack on Louza Police Station; police fired on demonstrators, killing and wounding a number of Chinese. Volunteers called out. Further street disturbances followed by general strike and anti-British boycott. Chinese Advisory Committee to S.M.C. resigned. Strikes ended in September. International judicial inquiry by American,

British and Japanese judges in October.

1926, April 14: Adoption by Ratepayers' meeting of resolution approving addition of three Chinese members to Municipal Council.

1926, July: Nationalists, organizing in Canton, launch military expedition to North, sweeping through Central China to Hankow. British return concessions at Hankow and Kiukiang to Chinese. Shanghai apprehensive of Nationalist advance.

1927, January 1: Rendition of Mixed Court and establishment of Provisional Court.

1927, February: Nationalists begin advance down Yangtsze Valley toward Shanghai.

1927, Jan.-Feb.-March: British, American, French, Spanish, Italian, and Japanese troops landed in Shanghai for defence of Settlement and Concession.

1927, March 21: Municipal Council declared State of Emergency. Volunteers called out. Nationalists occupied Chinese City. Fighting near Settlement during March resulted in defeat of Northern (anti-Nationalist) Forces, of whom 3,000 were interned in Settlement.

1927, July 7: City Government of Greater Shanghai established and Mayor appointed, placing Chinese territory surrounding Settlement and Concession under municipal form of government.

1928, April 20: Three Chinese Councillors first took their seats in Municipal Council.

1928, June 1: Public parks opened to Chinese on same terms as foreigners.

1929, April 17: Ratepayers adopt resolution authorizing sale of Municipal Electricity Department; Shanghai Power Co. assumes operation.

1930, April 1: Rendition of Shanghai Provisional Court and establishment in Settlement of District Court and Branch High Court.

1930, May 2: Number of Chinese members on Municipal Council increased from three to five.

1931, September: Japanese launch military operations in Manchuria following dynamiting of railway line, beginning movement which eventuated in alienation of three northeastern provinces from Chinese and establishment of Manchukuo, with Henry Pu-yi, deposed Emperor of China (1911), as Emperor.

1932, January 28: Following anti-Japanese boycott activities and Sino-Japanese racial disorders in Hongkew district, and failure of Chinese military forces to heed their notification to withdraw from neighbourhood of Settlement boundaries, Japanese naval forces made direct attack against Chinese (19th Route Army) in the Chapei district. Great Britain and United States lodged protests with Japan. Furious fighting in Chapei. Volunteers mobilized and curfew law enforced in Settlement and Concession, requiring residents to be off streets from 10 p.m. until 4 a.m. Great Britain and, United States heavily reinforced garrisons and warships of powers stood by in Whangpoo.

1932, March 2: Nineteenth Route Army withdrew from Chapei in good order in quickly executed maneuver. Japanese advance to protect lines. Negotiations instituted.

1932, May 5: Sino-Japanese Armistice signed, terminating "undeclared war."

1932, May 31: Japan withdrew major share of military forces of occupation. Property loss in Chapei placed at $350,000,000.

CLASSIFIED BUSINESS DIRECTORY

The business houses listed below are recommended with confidence. Should visitors experience any difficulty in obtaining what they need, the publishers of this guidebooks will be glad to be of assistance. Telephone 13771 – The University Press, 160 Avenue Edward VII.

Aerated Waters
Watson's Mineral Water Co., 327 Kiangse Rd., *Tel. 12726,*.

Antiques
Art d'Orient, 969 Bubbling Well Rd., *Tel. 35003.*
Mai Li Lacquer & Antique Co., A261 Broadway
Peking Treasure Shop, 8a Central Arc., 49 Nanking Rd.,
    Tel. 17159.

Auto Accessories
Central Auto Supply Co., 411 av. Foch, *Tel. 84679.*
Foo Lai Tyre & Rubber Repair Co., 57-9 Park Rd., *Tel. 32039.*
Wei Hai Auto Supply Co., 485 Yu Yuen Road, *Tel. 20678.*

Auto Tailors
Chang Yung Kee, 481 av. Foch, *Tel. 72496.*
Tai Chong & Co., 943 Avenue Road.

Bankers
National Commercial Bank, Ltd., 230 Peking Rd., *Tel. 18170.*
Union Mobiliere, Societe Francaise de Banque et de Placements,
    35-37 av. Edward VII, *Tel. 82163.*

Batteries
Tung Ya Storage Battery Co., 68 Park Road.
Union & Co., 463-5 av. Foch, *Tel. 75588.*

Beauty Parlours

Andre's Beauty Shop, 745 Bubbling Well Rd., *Tel. 30808.*
Baptiste Beauty Parlour, 4 av. Dubail, *Tel 84399.*
Bond Street Salon, The Room 119, Palace Hotel, Tel. 18030.
Die Dame German Beauty Parlour, 258 Yu Yuen Rd., *Tel 20290.*
Don's Beauty Salon, 1200 Bubbling Well Rd.
Eugene Italian Beauty Parlour, 496 r. Bourgeat.
Eugenic Beauty Salon, Astor House Hotel, Whangpoo Rd.,
    Tel. 42255.
European Beauty Parlour, The, 230 N. Soochow Rd., *Tel. 40463.*
Figaro Beauty Parlour, 142 rte. des Soeurs.
German Beauty Parlour, 1626 Bubbling Well Rd., *Tel. 34045.*
Gff Hwa Beauty Parlour, Nanking Rd., er. Kweichow Rd.
Institute de Beaute, 1209-11 Bubbling Well Rd., *Tel 32720.*
La Donna Bella Beauty Salon, 1481 Bubbling Well Rd.,
    Tel. 95721.
Liu & Co., Y. Y., 8 Carter Rd. *Tel. 95721.*
Maison Ando, 868 av. Joffre, *Tel. 72476.*
Mary's Beauty Parlour, 310 av. du Roi Albert, *Tel. 72585.*
Simen's Beauty Parlour, 698 av. Joffre, *Tel 74800.*
Verette Institute de Beaute., Mme., 17B Central Arcade,
    49 Nanking Rd., *Tel. 15972.*
Vienna Beauty Parlour, 696 av. Joffre, *Tel. 73863.*

Booksellers & Stationers

Evans & Sons, Ltd., Edward, 20,0 Kiukiang Rd., *Tel. 15015.*
Liu & Co., Y. Y., 8 Carter Rd.

Butchers

Asia Butchery, 1668 Bubbling Well Rd., *Tel. 32013.*
Continental Butchery Co., 1711 Bubbling Well Rd., *Tel. 32296.*
Dong Hing Butchery, 20-22 Carter Rd., *Tel. 31325.*
Godfrey & Co., 1202 Bubbling Well Rd., *Tel. 32936.*
Grand Market, 945 Yu Yuen Rd., *Tel. 20181.*
Nanyang Butchery, 26-30 r. de Say Zoong, *Tel. 71319.*
National Green Grocery & Co., 366-8 av. Joffre, *Tel. 83135.*
New Hopkin's Butchery, 2 r. Urge Maresea, *Tel. 71114.*
New State Market, 961 av. Joffre, *Tel. 72212.*
Shanghai Butchery Co., 9,0 Broadway, *Tel. 41009.*
Union Provision Co., 4-8 r. Kahn, *Tel. 73804.*
Universal Butchery, 63E Edinburgh Rd., *Tel. 21017*
Wah Vang Butchery Co., 1244 av. Joffre, *Tel. 70930.*
Welcome Butchery, 1269 Avenue Rd.

Cafes

Bianchi, C., 72 Nanking Rd., *Tel. 12264.*
Cafe Bonheur, 358 Chapoo Rd.
Cafe Restaurant, V. M. Altman, 752 av. Joffre, *Tel. 75472.*
Chang Kee Cafe, 583 av. Foch.
Little Cafe, 741 Bubbling Well Rd., *Tel. 34827.*
Palais Cafe, 57 av. Edward VII, *Tel. 81551.*
Vienna Ball Room, Bubbling Well Rd., *Tel. 31577.*

Canned Goods

Sun Sun Co., Ltd., 470 Nanking Rd., *Tel. 94118.*
Tai Kong Canned Provision Co., 377 Nanking Rd., *Tel. 94805.*

Carved-wood Furniture
George & Co., J. L., 805 Avenue Rd., *Tel. 34732.*
Sung Chong & Co., Ltd., 723 Bubbling Well Rd., *Tel. 33580.*
Wong Sun Tai, 42,5 Min-kuo Rd., North Gate,
  Tel. 23745 (Nantao).
Yung Shing Zung, 23 rte. de Say Zoong, *Tel. 72216.*

China & Earthenware
Tung Tuck & Co., 431 Min-kuo Rd., *Tel. 82687.*
Zing Chang Sing Co., 481 Middle Republic Rd.

Children's Outfitters
Kiddy Shop, The, 1005 Bubbling Well Rd., *Tel. 34974.*

Clairvoyante
Soloha, Madam, 1025 Bubbling Well Rd., 12A Wah Kee Av,
  Tel. 30529.

Coal Merchants
Tung Ho Coal Co., 494 rte. Vallon.
Zung Tai Co., 1058 Yu Yuen Rd.

Cold Storage
Ewo Cold Storage Co., 1500 Yangtszepoo Rd., *Tel. 50072.*

Cookery
Lewis Ideal School of Electric Cookery. The, Flat 250, 410
  Szechuen Rd.

Dr. P. T. CHEN, M.D., M.M.Sc. (Univ. of Penn.)*
Specialist in Urinary and Venereal Diseases
110 Sun Bldg., 505 Honan Rd.   Telephone 94499

Curios

Brothers Store, 549 Boul. des 2 Republiques.

Chuan Koo Chai, 53 Kiangse Rd.

Coral Island, 695 Hankow Rd., *Tel. 95328.*

Dong Kong & Co., 238 Yates Rd.

Fu Zung Tsai Jade Store, 285 Boul. les 2 Republiques,
    Tel. 82746.

Hua Mei & Co., 265 Yates Rd.

King Ven Chie, 47 Red House, Kiangse Rd.

Komai, S., Damascene Works, 298 Bubbling Well Rd.,
    Tel. 30570.

Little Shop, The, 272 Kiangse Rd., *Tel. 16580.*

Peking City, 355 Yates Rd.

Peking Treasure Shop. 8a Central Arc. 49 Nanking Rd.,
    Tel. 17159.

Saey Vung Tsar, 287 Boul. des 2 Republiques, *Tel. 82772.*

Tseng Yu Hsien, Foochow Curio Shop, 94 Pakai Lane,
    Min-kuo Rd. (Nantao).

Tung Koo Tsar, 262 Boul. des 2 Republiques, *Tel. 82442.*

Wang Tsung Lee Curio Store, 543 Min-kuo Rd., North Gate,
    (Nantao).

Yah Toong & Co., 529 Min-kuo Rd. (Nantao).

Ye Pao Chai & Co., 250 Yates Rd.

Ziu Ching Curio Company, 533 Boul. des 2 Republiques.

Customs Brokers & Packers

McGill & Co., Ltd., James, 120 Kiangse Rd., *Tel. 11284.*

Dairies

Model Dairy Farm, The, 8 Tifeng Rd., *Tel. 21997.*
Steys Dairy Farm & Ice Factory Co., Ltd., 92 Edinburgh Rd.,
    Tel. 20241.
Sung Sung Dairy, 175 G. Western Rd., *Tel. 20486.*
Yah Shing Dairy, 78 Tunsin Rd., *Tel. 20449.*

Dancing Academies

Jimmy's Dancing School, 1.17 Nanking Rd.
May's Dancing Academy, Shanghai Continental Bldg.,
    495 Honan Rd.
Waldemar's Dancing Academy, 1272 av. Joffre.
    Tel. 74292.

Delicatessen

Savoy Delicatessen Store, 131A rte. de Say Zoong, *Tel. 73371.*

Dentists

Ching Sau Wah & Sons, Drs., 121 Broadway, *Tel. 41927.*
John Hoh, Dr., King Yun Building, 378 Peking Rd.
Kormilitzina, Dr. L. K., 17B Central Arc., 49 Nanking Rd.,
    Tel. 15972.
Lews, Dr. T. P., Canton Dental Hospital, 975 N. Szechuen Rd.,
    Tel. 40204.
Shanghai Dental Mfg. Co., The, 123 Kweichow Rd., *Tel. 90921.*
Shao, Dr. W. Z., 17 Broadway, *Tel. 40509.*
Woo, Dr. D. C., Room 229, 128 Museum Rd., *Tel. 13398.*

Department Stores

Association for Domestic Industry, The, 191-3 Nanking Rd.,
    Tel. 90363.
Shanghai Co-operative Society, 611 av. Joffre, *Tel. 83069.*
Sun Sun Co., Ltd., 470 Nanking Rd., *Tel. 94118.*
Wing On Co. (Shanghai), Ltd., 551 Nanking Rd., *Tel. 90113.*

Dog Hospitals

Blue Cross Dog Hospital, 170 Edinburgh Rd., *Tel. 21193.*
Dog Hospital, 664 r. Lafayette.

Drapers & Haberdashers

Baranovsky, L., 850 ay. Joffre, *Tel. 73309.*
Emporium, The, 359 Yates Rd., *Tel. 31175.*
Grigorieff & Co.. P., 860 av. Joffre, *Tel. 72923.*
Jorloyork Trading 4@o., 69 Love Lane, *Tel. 75628.*
Otto Thate, 139 av. Haig, *Tel. 74581.*
Sun Sun Co., Ltd., 470 Nanking Rd., *Tel. 94118.*

Dressmakers

Georgette Gown & Hat Shoppe, 821 av. Joffre, *Tel. 73351.*
La Parisienne, 304 Yates Rd.
Little Madame, The, 312 r. Cardinal Mercier, *Tel. 72741.*
Maison Honorine, 662 av. Joffre, *Tel. 71615.*
Maison Lucile, 813 av. Joffre, *Tel. 72202.*
Modes de Reval, 262 Yu Yuen Rd., *Tel. 28746.*
Salon Mme. Gick, 1121 Bubbling Well Rd., *Tel. 34794.*
Yung Shing, 89 av. du Roi Albert, *Tel. 74802.*

Dry Cleaners & Dyers

Dah Yung Hwa Cleaning & Dyeing Works, 1034 Yu Yuen Rd.,
    Tel. 20072.
Fook Tah Co., C., 19 rte. de Say Zoong.
Great Western Dry Cleaning Co., The, 1246 av. Joffre, *Tel. 70801.*
Hamburg Dry Cleaning & Dyeing Co., 817 Avenue Rd.,
    Tel. 33040.

Hongkong & Co., 245 Yu Yuen Rd., *Tel. 20936.*
Hop Hsing & Co., 332 r. Cardinal Mercier, *Tel. 74786.*
John Hsing Co., The, 1258 av. Joffre, *Tel. 75085.*
Mei Hwa Hsing & Co., 495 Sinza Rd.
Savoy Dry Cleaning Co., The, 129 r. de Say Zoong, *Tel. 74623.*
Star Cleaning & Dyeing Service, The, 149 Hart Rd.
Tryit Co., The, 620 Yu Yuen Rd.
Wah Sung & Co., 728 Connaught Rd.
Washington Dry Cleaning & Dyeing Co., 103 Yates Rd.,
    Tel. 35323.
Welcome Dry Cleaning Co., 793-5 Great Western Rd., *Tel. 20352.*

Electrical Supplies

Bee Lee Electrical & Plumbing Supply Co., 1556 Avenue Rd.,
    Tel. 35250.
Chien Hwa Electric Supply Co., 393 av. Foch, *Tel. 83324.*
King Loong Electric & Sanitary Co.,2 Carter Rd., *Tel. 31632.*
New Light & Sanitary Co., 474 av. Foch, *Tel, 32330.*
Wukiang Electric & Water Supply Co., 10-12 rte. G. Kahn,
    Tel. 70308.
Zung Chong & Co., 750 Burkill Rd.

Electroplating

Roche & Co., 99-101 Love Lane, *Tot. 33562.*

Enamelware

Hwa Foong Enamelling Co., Ltd., 60-62 r. Port du Nord,
    Tel. 82036.

Engineers, General

Hsin Hung Chong Engineering Works, Ltd., Lane 273,
    80 Kiaochow Rd., *Tel. 33032.*

Bullion Brokers

Matao Yui, 60 Kiukiang Rd., *Tel. 14245.*

Fancy Goods

China Arts, 324 Yates Rd.

Komai. S., Damascene Works, 298 Bubbling Well Rd.,
Tel. 30574.

Marui & Co., 1609 Bubbling Well Rd.,
Tel. 35719.

Peking Jewellery Co., 329 Yates Rd., Tel. 34469.

Peking Treasure Shop, Sa Central Are., 49 Nanking Rd.,
Tel 17159.

Sun Sun Co., Ltd., 470 Nanking Rd., Tel. 94118.

Flowers

Avenue Joffre Flower Shop, The, 852 av. Joffre, Tel. 72185.

China Flower Shop, 832 Yu Yuen Rd.

Hongkong Flower Shop, 998 av. Joffre.

Lewis Nurseries, 412 Szechuen Rd., Tel. 14398.

Fruit

Kung Tai & Co., 953 av. du Roi Albert.

Furniture & Furnishings

Arts & Quality Co., 1595 Bubbling Well Rd.

Cathay Studio, 265 r. Cardinal Mercier, Tel. 75323.

Charming Artistic Furniture Co., 50-4 rte. des Soeurs, Tel. 72934.

Ching Chong Furnishing Co., 1072-4 Avenue Rd., Tel. 34749.

Full House Furnishing Co., J153 rte. des Soeurs, Tel. 75655.

Hwa Fo Furnishing Co., 1533 Bubbling Well Rd., Tel. 32786.

Mai Luji Arts Furniture Co., 131-3 rte. des Soeurs, Tel. 72643.

Modern Home, The, 874 Bubbling Well Rd., *Tel. 34310.*
Shanghai Decorating Co., The, Y375 N. Szechuen Rd.,
    Tel. 45204.
Shing Chong & Co., 381-3 Yu Yuen Rd.
Sung Furniture Co., 684 Bubbling Well Rd, *Tel. 33399.*
Tai Loong & Co., 873-5 Bubbling Well Rd., *Tel. 35694.*
Tiny & Co., 805 Bubbling Well Rd.
Vee Sing Furniture Co., 276 rte. de Say Zoong, *Tel. 71113.*
Way Shing Co., 409 ave. Foch.
Wong Zung Tai, 70 rte. de Say Zoong, *Tel. 37198.*
Yong Chong Furnishers & Decorators Co., 1017 Yates Rd.,
    Tel. 34612.
Yuan Tai Furniture Co., 59 Avenue Rd.
Tang & Co., S.F., 1605 Bubbling Well Rd., *Tel. 35105.*

Furs
Chan Kee Fur Co., 465 Szechuen Rd., *Tel. 17287.*
International Fur Co., 775 Bubbling Well Rd.

Garages & Auto Repair Shops
General Auto Service, 1881-7 Avenue Rd.
Isaacs Motor Service, 368A Taku Rd., *Tel. 32121.*
Min Chung Motor Repairing Works Co., A755 Avenue Pd.
Mitchell's, T. L., Motor Service, 112D Edinburgh Rd., *Tel. 21108.*
Perfect Motor Service, 112-4 Park Rd., *Tel. 95191.*
Reo Co., 367-9 Weihaiwei Rd., *Tel. 34129.*
Standard Auto Service, 18 r. Amiral Courbet, *Tel. 70670.*
United Motor Co., 855 Avenue Rd., *Tel. 32449.*

Gifts
Bon Voyage Gift Shop, Sassoon Arc., Nanking Rd., *Tel. 13289.*
Peking Treasure Shop, 8a Central Are., 49 Nanking Rd.,
    Tel. 17159.

Greengrocers
American Vegetable Store, 1253 Bubbling Well Rd., *Tel. 35203.*
San Francisco Vegetable Store, 1698 Bubbling Well Rd..
   Tel. 31591.

Groceries & Provisions
Chun Lee, 17 Siking Rd., *Tel. 13878.*
Dah Yuen Provision Store, 1711-3 Bubbling Well Rd., *Tel. 33376.*
Dombey & Son, Ltd., 893 Bubbling Well Rd., *Tel. 30641.*
Hung Kong Provision Store, 1652-4 Bubbling Well Rd.
Paramount Store, The, 1539 Bubbling Well Rd., *Tel. 34311.*
Sanitary Provision Co., Ltd., 748-52 ay. Joffre, *Tel. 73218.*
Shanghai Food Supply, 323 r. Bourgeat, *Tel. 72040.*
Shanghai General Supply Co., 1843-5 av. Joffre, *Tel. 70307.*
Shing Kee & Co., 1254 Avenue Rd., *Tel. 33081.*
Sun Sun Co., Ltd., 420 Nanking Rd., *Tel. 94118.*
Yih Lee Hong, 1.153 rte. des Soeurs.
Van Shing & Co., 955-7-9 av. Joffre, *Tel. 73595.*
Yuen Tao & Co., 241 av. Haig, *Tel. 74098.*

Hairdressers
Nanking Barber Shop, The, 784 Bubbling Well Rd., *Tel. 32958.*
Palace Hairdressing Saloon, 567 Nanking Rd., *Tel. 93552.*
Yokohama Barber Shop, 263 Kiangse Rd.

Hardware
Espero & Co., 30 Carter Rd.
Shin Chong Yih & Co., 17-21 Kiangse Rd., *Tel. 19361.*
Tsepin, V., 656 av. Joffre, *Tel. 73733.*

Hire Cars
Dah Hwa Garage Co., 313 Seymour Rd., *Tel. 30711.*
Kung Woo Yah Kee Garage, 405 Gordon Rd., *Tel. 34142.*
Nanking Garage Ho Kee Co., Ltd., 157 Moulmein Rd.,
   Tel. 35960.

Morimura Garage, S.96A Fearon Rd., *Tel. 41730.*
New York Garage Ho Kee Co., 29-31 r. des Soeurs, *Tel. 72944.*
Shanghai Yai Kee Garage Co., 441-3 Boul. de Montigny,
　　Tel. 81291.
Taylor Garage, 96 r. Cardinal Mercier, *Tel. 70050.*

Hotels
Far Eastern Hotel, Ltd., 90 Thibet Rd., *Tel. 94030.*
New Asia Hotel, Ltd., cr. North Szechuen Rd. & Tiendong Rd.,
　　Tel. 42210.

Ice
Roo Ching Kee Ice Co., 626 Yu Yuen Rd., *Tel. 20480.*

Importers & Commission Agents
Chafock & Co., 159 Canton Rd., *Tel 19962.*

Jade
Jade Bazaar, 61 Kiangse Rd.
Juen Chi, The, 343 Yates Rd.

Jewellers & Silversmiths
Peking Jewellery Co., 329 Yates Rd., *Tel. 34469.*
Peking Treasure Shop, Sa Central Are., 49 Nanking Rd.,
　　Tel. 17159.
Stepanoff, G., 800 ay. Joffre, *Tel. 71845.*
Tuck Chang & Co., Ltd., 67 Broadway, *Tel. 42923.*
Zee Wo & Co., 370 Honan Rd.

Laces & Lace Goods
China Lace Factory, The, 159-61 Canton Rd., *Tel. 16608.*
King Zeng Kee Lace Co., 9 Central Rd., *Tel. 11812.*
Wee Lee & Co., M. W., 823 Avenue Rd.

Lampshades
Tang Zung Kee & Co., 817-9 Bubbling Well Rd., *Tel. 33248.*
Zung Chong & Co., 750 Burkill Rd.

Leather Goods
Everlast Trunk Factory, 370 Thibet Rd.
Sun Sun Co., Ltd., 470 Nanking Rd., *Tel. 94118.*
Swan Leather Piece Goods Co., 36 Broadway.
Waling Trunk Co.. 490 ay. Joffre, *Tel. 81796.*
World Trunk Co., Factory, Thibet Rd., er. Kiukiang Rd.,
    Tel. 90299.

Linens & Linen Goods
Cathay Arts Co., 103 Central Arcade, Nanking Rd., *Tel. 11858.*
Peking Treasure Shop, Sa Central Are., 49 Nanking Rd.,
    Tel. 17159.

Lingerie
Peking Treasure Shop, Sa Central Arc., 49 Nanking Rd.,
    Tel. 17159.

Livery Stables
Zung Kee Livery Stable, Cr. Lincoln Av. and Chungshan Rd.,
    Tel. 21223.

Massage
Francis, Madani, 4 Astor Terrace, Astor Rd.
Medical Massage Clinic, F.2 Chinai Rd., er. Love Lane,
    Tel. 35469.
Mrs. Nona, 106 Range Rd.

Millinery
Hamilton, Mme., 287 av. du Roi Albert, *Tel. 70639.*

Music Stores
Robinson Piano Co., Ltd., 77 Nanking Rd., *Tel. 10868.*
Suchochleb, Alois. 47 Seward Rd., *Tel. 40344.*

Opticians
National Optical Co., The, 163 Nanking Rd., *Tel. 91224.*
Oriental Optical Co., The, 246 Canton Rd., *Tel. 15456.*

Painters & Decorators
Yang Shing Kee, 105 Yu Yuen Rd., *Tel. 27480.*

Pets
Shanghai Pet Store, 744 Dixwell Rd. & 1533 Bubbling Well

Pharmacies
Help Pharmacy, 1052 Yu Yuen Rd., *Tel. 20147.*
Regal Pharmacy, 1180 Bubbling Well Rd., *Tel. 30310.*
Star Pharmacy, 837 av. Joffre, *Tel. 71810.*
Tunik's Pharmacy, E. B., 263 av. Haig, *Tel. 75241.*
Union Pharmacy, 760 av. Joffre, *Tel. 73632.*
Vita Pharmacy, 783 Bubbling Well Rd., *Tel. 35520.*

Photographers
Lee Bros., 1959 Bubbling Well Rd.
Ng-Ngo Sheng, 47 Thibet Rd.
Porter Photo Co., 258 Bubbling Well Rd., *Tel. 30258.*
Suzuki, Y., 872 N. Szechuen Rd.
Tohyama, T., 169 Haining Rd., *Tel. 41634.*
Wong Photo Studio, C. H., 308 Nanking Rd., *Tel. 91245.*
Yoshisaka Photo Co., 92-94 Chapoo Rd., *Tel. 40271.*

Photographic Supplies
Hwa Chong Photo Supplies Co., 345 Shantung Rd., *Tel. 93225.*
Standard Photo Supply Co., 375 Nanking Rd., *Tel. 92473.*

Physicians
Chow, Dr. M. Z., 544 Szechuen Rd., *Tel. 19766.*
Howard, Dr. George, 979 N. Szechuen Rd.
Lew, Dr. George, 96, Lane 12, Bubbling Well Rd., *Tel. 92461.*
Lin, Dr. S. H., 420 Continental Emporium Bldg., Nanking Rd.,
  Tel. 91122.
Tsin-Sung Kiang, Dr., Land Bank Bldg., 255 Peking Rd.,
  Tel. 13992.
Yang, Dr. V. M., 536 Szechuen Rd., *Tel. 19185.*

Piece Goods
Yali Sing Chong & Co., 257 Yates Rd., *Tel. 32214*

Postage Stamps
Katkofr, A. A., 1413 Avenue Rd.

Poultry & Eggs
Pootung Fowls Farm, 19B rte. de Say Zoong, *Tel. 725700.*

Printers & Publishers
University Press, The, 160 av. Edward VII, *Tel. 13771.*

Pulverized Stone
Shun Chang Stone Pulv. Works, Line 1034, Z14 Cordon Rd.,
  Tel. 34210.

Radio Supplies
Shanghai Radio Engineering Co., 49 Nanking Rd., *Tel. 14996.*

Railways
Nanking-Shanghai & Shanghai-Hangchow-Ningpo Railways
Adm., Pass. & Goods Dept., 407 Bubbling Well Rd.,
Tel. 35815.

Rattan Goods
May Shing Rattan Co., 127-9 site. des Soeurs, *Tel. 73049.*
Tsai Zung Shing, Lane 664, 7 Hart Rd.
Shanghai Arts, 994-6 Gt. Western Rd.

Real Fstate
Moeller & Co., L. E., 110, Szechuen Rd., *Tel. 16650.*
Realty Investment Co., 210 Szechuen Rd., *Tel. 18625.*
Ya Loong Realty & Land Investment Co., 24 Love Lane,
Tel. 34091.

Refrigerators
Refrigerator Service Co., 253 av. Haig, *Tel. 74078.*

Rugs
China Rug Co., Ltd., 481 Bubbling Well Rd., *Tel. 35272.*
Golden Dragon Rug Co., 417 Bubbling Well Rd., *Tel. 34943.*
Golden Star Rug Co., 747 Bubbling Well Rd., *Tel. 32706.*
Pagoda Rug Co., 505 Bubbling Well Rd., *Tel. 33380.*
Peking Treasure Shop, 8a Central Are., 49 Nanking Rd.,
Tel. 17159.
Tab Yiu Art Rug Shop, 12 Yates Rd., *Tel. 34892.*

Saddlers
Chu Lee Ziang, B50 Gt. Western Rd., *Tel. 28255.*

Sculpture
Wagstaff Studio, W. W., 118 Gt. Western Rd., *Tel. 20911.*

Shirtmakers

Fujiwara Shirt Co., 79 Boone Rd., *Tel. 43269.*
King Sei, 596 Woosung Rd., *Tel. 41384.*
Peace & Co., H. S., 66 Boone Rd., *Tel. 40904.*
Yu Ning, W., Shirttmaker. 392 Haining Rd., *Tel. 41877.*

Shoes

Alexander Shoe Co.. 9 Nanking Rd., *Tel. 10786.*
Beauty Shoe Co., 5 Yates Rd.
Dah Yung Hwa and Pacific Shoe Co., 1034 Yu Yuen Rd.
Hwa Foong Co., 36 Carter Rd.
Kiang San Shoe Co., 296 Yu Yuen Rd.
Lightfoot Shoe Co., 722 av. Joffre.
Uyeda Shoe Co., 127 av. Haig.

Silk

Great China Silk Co., 229-35 Yates Rd., *Tel. 35779.*
King Kong, 349 Yates Rd.
My Chong Co., 340 Yates Rd.
Yah Sing Chong & Co., 207 Yates Rd.

Sporting Goods

Mackenzie Sports Co., 753 Bubbling Well Rd., *Tel. 35355.*
Shih L. Co., C. L., 681 Bubbling Well Rd.

Steamship Companies

Chang On Steamship Co., Lane 14, B2 Kiangse Rd.,
   Tel. 19437.

China Merchants' S.N. Co., Ltd., 9 The Bund, *Tel. 11589.*
North-China Steamship Co., Ltd., 29 r. du Consulat,
    Tel. 81388.

Tailors, Gents
Bent Brothers It Co., 155-761 Bubbling Well Rd., *Tel. 32390.*
Chang Seng, 613 Nanking Rd., *Tel. 91332.*
Heng Kong My Tailor, 563 Szechuen Rd., *Tel. 12205.*
Hie Kang, 996-998 Avenue Rd.
Mei Tai, 718 Weihaiwei Rd.
Wei Lee & DSB, 464 N. Szechuen Rd., *Tel. 46541.*
Wal Kong Co., 226-30 Thibet Rd., *Tel. 91542.*

Tailors, Ladies (see also "Dressmakers")
Fook Tab, 19 rte. de Say Zoong.
Hang Sun, 1640, Avenue Rd.
Henry, Ladies' Tailor, 2 rte. Paul Henry.
Hong Chong, 298 Yates Rd.
Hong Shin, 334 Yates Rd., *Tel. 33569.*
Hong Shing Kee, 328 Yates Rd.
King Foo Kee, 479-499 Hart Rd.
Kin Chong, 286 Yates Rd., *Tel. 33201.*
Mei Fah, C., 1450M Avenue Rd.
Modern Tailor, 115 av. du Roi Albert, *Tel. 74327*
Nee Kee, E19 rte. do Say Zoong, *Tel. 71282.*
Sing Kong, 698 Rue Lafayette.
Sun Chong Co., 32C, Yates Rd.
Sun Tai, 256 Yates Rd.
Tuck Chong, 354 Yates Rd.
Woo Tai, 85 av. du Roi Albert, *Tel. 74802.*
Yah Woo, V278 Yates Rd.
Yao Lee, 330 Yates Rd.
Yong Kee. 50-52 Yates Rd.
Young Hsing, 89 av. du Roi Albert.
Yun Kee & Co., 1642 Avenue Rd.

Tea

Chung Sing Chong, 51 Museum Rd., *Tel. 18376.*

Underwear

China A.B.C. Underwear Weaving Mill, Ltd., 472 Nanking Rd., *Tel. 94431.*
Chine Tai Underwear Co., 353 Yates Rd., *Tel. 30629.*
Hsin Tai, V280 Yates Rd.
Loo Brothers, 368 Yates Rd., *Tel. 31924.*
Loen Tai Underwear Co., Ltd., 358 Yates Rd.
Mow Kee, 338 Yates Rd.
Oriental Star Underwear Co., L110, 3 Chapoo Rd., *Tel. 43472.*

Upholsterers

Lee Tai, 652 Yu Yuen Rd.
Pure, Jacob, 50 Gt. Western Rd.
Van Tai Tailors, 62 rte. de Say Zoong.
Wah Tai Tailor, 59 Dah Sze Rd.

Vulcanizing

Oriental Vulcanizing Co., 579 av. Foch, *Tel. 71949.*

Wallpaper

Hollywood Wall Paper Co., 486 av. Joffre, *Tel. 32552.*

Wines & Spirits

Ramsay & Co., N. B., 24 Nanking Rd., *Tel. 10139.*

Woollen Goods

Mareel Depot, 49 Nanking Rd.

Wrought Iron-Work

Modern Workshop, 585 Bubbling Well Rd.

Coming Back?

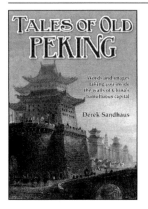
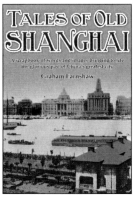
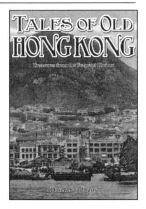

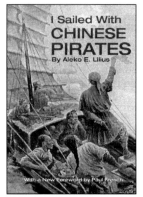
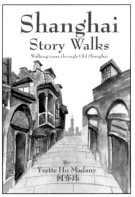

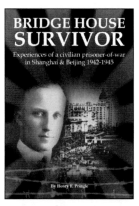
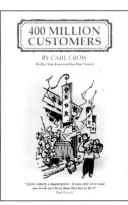